STORIES, SONGS, and STRETCHES!

ALA Editions purchases fund advocacy, awareness, and accreditation programs for library professionals worldwide.

STORIES, SONGS, and STRETCHES!

Creating Playful Storytimes with Yoga and Movement

KATIE SCHERRER

An imprint of the American Library Association
Chicago 2017

KATIE SCHERRER spends her time in the library and the yoga worlds, and she loves it when the two come together! Formerly a children's librarian, Katie is known for her consulting and training work helping libraries and educational organizations improve services to Latino immigrant communities through outreach and bilingual programming. She is also a Registered Yoga Teacher (RYT). Since 2013, Katie has been teaching yoga to children in many settings, including libraries, yoga studios, and schools. Katie graduated summa cum laude from Capital University (Ohio) in 2004, traveled the world, fell in love with yoga and libraries, and received her Master of Library and Information Science (MLIS) degree from Kent State University in 2009. She is the coauthor of *Once Upon a Cuento: Bilingual Storytime in English and Spanish,* published by ALA Editions. To learn more about Katie's work, or to schedule an online or in-person training session with her, please visit www.connectedcommunitiesconsulting.com and www.katiescherreryoga.com.

© 2017 by the American Library Association

Extensive effort has gone into ensuring the reliability of the information in this book; however, the publisher makes no warranty, express or implied, with respect to the material contained herein.

ISBN: 978-0-8389-1544-8 (paper)

Library of Congress Cataloging-in-Publication Data
Names: Scherrer, Katie, author.
Title: Stories, songs, and stretches! : creating playful storytimes with yoga and movement / Katie Scherrer.
Description: Chicago : ALA Editions, an imprint of the American Library Association, 2017. | Includes bibliographical references.
Identifiers: LCCN 2016047209 | ISBN 9780838915448 (pbk. : alk. paper)
Subjects: LCSH: Children's libraries—Activity programs—United States. | Libraries and preschool children—United States. | Yoga—Study and teaching (Preschool)—Activity programs.
Classification: LCC Z718.3 .S393 2017 | DDC 027.62/5—dc23 LC record available at https://lccn.loc.gov/2016047209

⊚ This paper meets the requirements of ANSI/NISO Z39.48–1992 (Permanence of Paper).

Printed in the United States of America

21 20 19 18 17   5 4 3 2 1

To my yin and yang mentors, Toni Reiss and Libby Alexander.
Thank you for helping me find my way.

Contents

Introduction

How are you feeling, right now, as you pick up this book and begin to look through it? Perhaps you notice excitement about the idea of incorporating yoga into your storytime programs. Perhaps there is skepticism about the role of yoga in a library setting or for this particular age group. Perhaps you like the idea of making your storytime programs more physically active but feel a little uncertain about how to start. Maybe you're just curious. Whatever you are feeling, try right now just to notice it, with as little judgment as possible. Whether you love yoga, hate it, or are ambivalent toward it, just notice these as passing thoughts, the way you would notice fluffy clouds moving through a bright blue sky. Notice if there are any physical sensations that accompany your thoughts, paying particular attention to the sensations at the jaw, the shoulders, across the chest, and in the stomach. If you encounter any sensations of gripping or tightness, is it possible to soften in those areas? What effects do you experience in the mind when you allow the body to relax in this way? Just notice. No matter your experience with or opinion of yoga, you are invited now to suspend your judgment and explore this work with an open mind.

Yoga is a contemplative movement practice that people have been using for thousands of years, first in India and now in all corners of the globe, to deepen their self-awareness, improve their physical health, and reduce their experience of stress. As one of my yoga teacher friends often says, "Yoga changes us, and yoga keeps us exactly the same." What she means is that many people find that the practice of yoga helps them feel relaxed and confident, allowing their true selves to shine brightly as they find some of their unnecessary or unhelpful habits beginning to drop away. As you explore this manual, you may find that it encourages you to change your storytime—and keep it the same. This work is not intended to present a radical new approach to designing and implementing preschool storytime, abandoning the early literacy practices and other traditions that characterize storytimes across the country and beyond. As you read with an open mind, you will find that this work presents yoga and movement as tools that librarians and others can use intentionally to engage children and families through embodied play. This work honors and builds upon traditional storytime, as it presents new ideas for using a millennia-old movement practice to enhance it.

This work is written specifically for public librarians working in youth services departments and presenting storytime programs to preschool-age audiences. However, its use is not limited to the library setting. Early childhood educators may discover ideas for incorporating yoga and movement into their circle times or daily transitions. Children's yoga teachers may use it to deepen their understanding of child development and broaden their exposure to high-quality children's literature. Finally, parents and caregivers may glean some ideas for how to share yoga at home with their young children in a fun and engaging way.

This book begins with a discussion of yoga and how it has changed over the centuries. It dispels common myths or misunderstandings about yoga and moves on to discuss the evidence-based benefits of yoga to adults and children. Guidance is given on how to locate a qualified children's yoga teacher to lead library programming, if necessary. Chapter 2 dives more deeply into the benefits of the use of yoga and movement with preschool children, specifically exploring how yoga can support children's physical, social-emotional, and early literacy development. In chapter 3, step-by-step direction is provided regarding how to design and launch a yoga storytime program. Guidance is offered on general program design, materials selection, and the logistical arrangements of physical space, props, and marketing. A case study of librarians regularly offering a successful yoga storytime program in their library is shared. Chapter 4 presents thirteen basic yoga poses and more than two dozen variations of those poses, along with specific suggestions for how to use the poses in a yoga storytime setting to stimulate children's early learning. Chapter 5 offers a year's worth of monthly yoga storytime program plans, fully designed and ready to use. This work concludes with a list of professional materials and online resources to assist you in your yoga storytime planning. A complete bibliography of all materials used in the sample yoga storytime plans and suggested picture books for such programming are also included.

This work represents a unique culmination of my experience in two seemingly distant worlds, both of which have been central to my life for well over a decade. My library work embraces my passion for empowering diverse and traditionally underserved families through strategic outreach, creative partnerships, and culturally relevant programming. Over the years that I have been working in and with libraries, I have also been studying yoga and mindfulness. These practices have both changed me and kept me the same, allowing me to slowly release unhelpful patterns and come closer to my most authentic self. This process is a lifelong one; though I am a yoga teacher today, I am always a student first. Sharing yoga with children of all ages (from toddlers to teens) as a children's yoga instructor has kept me honest and dedicated to my own practice—those of us who work with children know that they sure can smell a fake! It has also made me an even more fervent supporter of public libraries and all they have to offer to families. All these experiences have come together to prepare me to write the book you are reading today.

It is my sincere hope that this work will inspire you to let your personality shine more fully in the storytimes you lead, regardless of whether you ever include a single yoga pose. I believe that our role as children's librarians is to facilitate *connection* for the families we serve—connection with books and reading, with the public library as an institution, and with one another. When we are authentic and present in our work, willing to connect *ourselves* with the families we serve, we create an environment in which it is possible for all these other connections to develop. Yoga storytime can be a special way in which to foster this connection, a program in which fun and creativity flow freely. Enjoy the journey.

Chapter One

An Introduction to Yoga

hat is yoga? This seemingly straightforward question can elicit a variety of responses, depending on who is asked. Based on one's experience and perspective, yoga may be thought of as a form of exercise, a spiritual practice, a fitness fad, a relaxation strategy, or an esoteric form of self-torture! Often, yoga is defined as a union of the body, heart, and mind; yoga is what we experience when these seemingly disparate parts of the self are brought together. In order to move forward in discussing how yoga can be used in the storytime setting, it is helpful to first understand a bit more about what yoga is and is not. The following section is intended to provide this context.

A Brief History of Yoga

Yoga is a contemplative movement practice that originated in ancient India, where it has been practiced for at least two thousand years.[1] The word *yoga* can be translated as "to yoke, join, or concentrate."[2] In the past, yoga was taught directly from one teacher to one student, mostly men. Great emphasis was placed on meditation. Physical practices were a means to purify and prepare the body to sit in meditation for long periods of time. Two of the most important historical yoga texts are the *Yoga Sutra,* credited to the Indian sage Patanjali, and the *Bhagavad-Gîtâ.*

MODERN YOGA

In the late 1800s, yoga masters from India began traveling to the West to share the practice. From that period on, the practice of yoga went through tremendous change. European gymnastics and an overall enthusiasm for health and physical strength prevalent in the early 1900s influenced yoga greatly. Teachers offered yoga as a system for full-body health, and their students began to demonstrate and teach their incredible feats of physical strength to large groups.[3] Western interest in Eastern philosophy also increased interest in yoga and influenced how it was taught to Westerners.[4] Perhaps the most influential teacher of this time was T. Krishnamacharya, whose students B. K. S. Iyengar (founder of the alignment-based Iyengar Yoga), K. Pattabhi Jois (founder of the intense vinyasa-style Ashtanga practice), Indra Devi (yoga teacher to Hollywood stars in the mid-1900s), and T. K. V. Desikachar (founder of Viniyoga) went on to have tremendous influence on the spread of yoga in the West.

YOGA TODAY

Today there is a yoga practice available for every body type and personality style, from fast-paced *vinyasa* classes to deeply relaxing restorative classes to yoga that has been adapted for special populations, such as senior citizens, pregnant women, and children. Yoga is typically taught in a group setting by a trained yoga teacher in a yoga studio, though with the rise of yoga's popularity, it is common to find classes being held today in gyms, community centers, public parks, and even libraries. Yoga classes commonly include yoga poses (*asana*), breathing practices (*pranayama*), meditation, and relaxation.

Yoga Myths

Perhaps the most important yoga myth to dispel is that yoga is a religion; it is not. Though the roots of yoga are those of a spiritual practice, today yoga is generally practiced in a completely secular manner. There is plenty of yoga philosophy available for interested students to explore and apply to their lives as desired, and some may find that yoga helps them develop or deepen their spiritual lives. However, many others simply enjoy the physical and mental benefits of the stretching and relaxation the practice offers. What a student takes away from a yoga practice is ultimately up to the individual.

Another pervasive yoga myth worth addressing is that one must be "flexible," possess a certain level of physical fitness, or look a certain way to practice yoga. This is not true. Yoga is indeed for everybody, and a qualified yoga teacher will know how to help students modify the practice to work best for their bodies. It doesn't matter if you can't yet (or ever!) touch your toes, or if you can easily press yourself up into a full backbend when you first step out of bed in the morning—yoga is for everyone.[5]

Yoga Benefits

Though not long ago considered "fringe" or "counterculture," yoga in the United States today is very much mainstream. Thirty-six million people are practicing yoga in the United States, and this number continues to increase year after year.[6] Over 28 percent of Americans have participated in a yoga class at some point in their lives, often citing physical health and stress reduction benefits as their motivators.[7] The scientific community has taken note of these claims of positive mental and physical benefits. Scientific research has found that practicing yoga can do the following:[8]

- Reduce back pain
- Reduce stress
- Lower heart rate and blood pressure
- Help relieve anxiety, depression, and insomnia
- Improve overall physical fitness, strength, and flexibility

Yoga and Preschool Children

A child's yoga is quite different from yoga for adults. Though many poses and practices are used in both adult and children's yoga settings, there is no expectation of precise form, rigorous flow, or extended silence in a child's practice. Yoga can be shared with children in a variety of contexts and by a variety of people, such as yoga teachers in studios, classroom teachers in schools, librarians in storytime, and parents or other caregivers at home.

As with adult yoga, yoga for children is becoming increasingly popular. A 2012 study found that 1.7 million children had practiced yoga in the previous year.[9] As with adult yoga practitioners, the number of children practicing yoga continues to rise annually.[10] Today, children are practicing yoga in over 940 schools across the United States.[11] Some researchers have wondered whether the benefits of an adult yoga practice are applicable to children as well as whether there are other benefits to children specific to their developmental stage. Though less quality research is available on the specific benefits of yoga for children, some studies have found that yoga can help children do the following:

- Improve self-regulation[12] (which is considered an important component of school readiness)
- Reduce the negative effects of stress and stress response[13]
- Promote attention and social skills[14]
- Improve endurance, strength, motor planning, motor performance, static balance, bilateral coordination, and flexibility[15]
- Improve cardiovascular health[16]

Research specific to yoga programs in school settings has found numerous positive benefits to children as well, including increased emotional balance, attentional control, and cognitive efficiency as well as reduced anxiety, negative thought patterns, reactivity, and negative behavior.[17] No studies have found adverse effects on children from practicing yoga, suggesting that yoga has a high safety profile.[18]

Children's Yoga Classes Compared with Yoga Storytime

Although a children's yoga class and a yoga storytime will be similar in many ways, they are not the same thing. The intentions of the two will be slightly different. The skills, knowledge, and training of the person leading the programs will be different as well. Let's take a look at the two in a bit more detail.

CHILDREN'S YOGA CLASSES

Teaching yoga to children in an age-appropriate manner is the key goal of a children's yoga class. Yoga classes for children can be offered in many settings, including yoga studios, fitness clubs, community centers, and even libraries. In a children's yoga class, yoga poses will be taught along with breathing practices, meditation, yoga philosophy, and the like. Teaching yoga to children requires specialized knowledge of anatomy, child development, yoga poses, and appropriate modifications for children. Therefore, children's yoga classes should be led by a credentialed yoga teacher who has specific training in the instruction of yoga to children.

YOGA STORYTIME

The goals of a yoga storytime, as with any storytime, are to engage children with books and language and to model practices that support early learning to adult caregivers. In a yoga storytime, yoga and movement are used as tools to help reach these goals; they are means rather than ends. Nearly anyone with the necessary skills and training required to lead professional storytimes for families and young children can add basic yoga poses and movement into their storytime programs. If you are presenting a yoga storytime, it is advisable that you have a regular yoga practice of your own in order to be comfortable moving your own body into the various yoga poses you are sharing with children. Be sure to clarify that you are not a yoga teacher, particularly if you receive questions from adults about yoga. Have a list of recommended children's yoga resources and local classes that you can give to families if they are interested in a more yoga-focused program than what you are offering.

HIRING A CHILDREN'S YOGA TEACHER

If you are interested in providing yoga classes for children at your library, or if you would like to offer a yoga storytime, but do not have any staff who are comfortable leading this style of programming, then you will need to hire a children's yoga teacher to present the program, either on her own or in cooperation with library staff. The following are some key points to look for when hiring a yoga teacher.

- *Appropriate yoga credentials.* Teaching yoga is not a highly regulated profession in the way other fields, such as medicine, are. In most states, anyone can call himself a yoga teacher, regardless of whether he has completed any training. That being said, Yoga Alliance (www.yogaalliance.org) is a nonprofit organization that works to regulate the industry. Most yoga studios require their teachers to have completed a minimum of two hundred hours of training at a Registered Yoga School (RYS) and to have undergone the process of registering with Yoga Alliance to become a Registered Yoga Teacher (RYT). Anyone using the RYT credential can be verified through the Yoga Alliance website. Someone who has obtained this credential has completed at least two hundred hours of training in the instruction of yoga; however, the amount of time spent learning about the instruction of yoga to children (if any) varies from program to program.

- *Specific training in teaching yoga to children.* Dozens of programs provide training in the instruction of yoga to children, including Childlight Yoga, Yoga Kids, Karma Kids Yoga, Rainbow Yoga, Little Flower Yoga, and many more. Yoga teachers who are already RYTs can complete an additional ninety-five hours of training specific to the instruction of yoga for children to obtain the Yoga Alliance designation of Registered Children's Yoga Teacher (RCYT). Someone who has obtained this credential has completed a minimum of two hundred hours of training in the instruction of yoga in general and an additional ninety-five hours of training just in the instruction of yoga to children. This certification is the gold standard for children's yoga teachers.
- *Experience working with children.* Experience can matter almost as much as training when it comes to teaching yoga to children. A Registered Yoga Teacher (RYT) may or may not be qualified to teach yoga to children, depending on her experience. When hiring a yoga teacher for kids, look for specific training in children's yoga instruction or experience working with children. Ideal children's yoga teachers will have a combination of both.
- *Liability insurance.* Professional yoga teachers are required by most yoga studios to carry their own liability insurance. Ask any yoga teacher you are considering hiring to supply proof of this insurance. In addition to providing extra protection to the library in the extremely low chance of an injury, being able to supply proof of this insurance is a mark of the teacher's professionalism.

If you are interested in hiring a teacher to teach yoga classes for kids at your library, look for someone who is either a certified children's yoga teacher through one of the many available children's yoga programs or a Registered Yoga Teacher (RYT) with experience teaching yoga to children. A Registered Children's Yoga Teacher (RCYT) is ideal but may be difficult to find. Depending on your area, expect to pay a rate of $30 to $75 for a forty-five-minute program.

Concluding Thoughts

Yoga is understood differently by different people. It is a contemplative movement practice that has changed greatly over time, spreading from its roots in ancient India to every corner of the globe. Today there are specific yoga practices available for all people, including children. As concerns regarding childhood obesity[19] and the effects of screen time[20] rise, yoga offers a healthy opportunity for children to engage in physical activity, learn strategies for self-regulation, and interact socially with other children and adults. As the next chapter will explore, yoga and storytime combined can be powerful for supporting young children in their early learning. Whether a storytime leader chooses to incorporate yoga on his own or decides to hire a qualified children's yoga teacher, the possibilities are unlimited for what a yoga storytime can look like in action and how it can help engage young children in body, heart, and mind.

NOTES

1. Gurjeet S. Birdee et al., "Clinical Applications of Yoga for the Pediatric Population: A Systematic Review," *Academic Pediatrics* 9, no. 4 (2009): 212.

2. Mara Carrico, "A Beginner's Guide to the History of Yoga," *Yoga Journal*. www.yoga journal.com/article/beginners/the-roots-of-yoga.

3. Joseph S. Atler, "Yoga, Bodybuilding, and Wrestling: Metaphysical Fitness," in *Yoga: The Art of Transformation*, ed. Debra Diamond (Washington, DC: Smithsonian Institution, 2013), 85–93.

4. Michelle Goldberg, *The Goddess Pose: The Audacious Life of Indra Devi, the Woman Who Helped Bring Yoga to the West* (New York: Knopf, 2015).

5. Contemporary yoga teachers like Jessamyn Stanley (http://jessamynstanley.com), an African American, queer yoga teacher based out of Durham, North Carolina, who self-describes as "fat-femme," are helping to dissolve the stereotype of the thin, white, cisgender female yoga practitioner.

6. Ipsos Public Affairs, Yoga Journal, and Yoga Alliance, *2016 Yoga in America Study* (January 2016), www.yogaalliance.org/Portals/0/2016 Yoga in America Study RESULTS.pdf.

7. Ibid.

8. National Center for Complementary and Integrative Health, "Yoga," https://nccih.nih .gov/sites/nccam.nih.gov/files/Yoga_for_Health_12-01-2015.pdf.

9. National Center for Complementary and Integrative Health, "Use of Complementary Health Approaches in the U.S.," https://nccih.nih.gov/research/statistics/NHIS/2012/ mind-body/yoga#child-data.

10. Ibid.

11. Bethany Butzer et al., "School-Based Yoga Programs in the United States: A Survey," *Advances* 29, no. 4 (2015): 18.

12. Rachel A. Razza, Dessa Bergen-Cico, and Kimberly Raymond, "Enhancing Preschoolers' Self-Regulation Via Mindful Yoga," *Journal of Child and Family Studies* 24, no. 2 (2015): 379.

13. Mark T. Greenberg and Alexis R. Harris, "Nurturing Mindfulness in Children and Youth: Current State of Research," *Child Development Perspectives* 6, no. 2 (2012): 163.

14. Razza, Bergen-Cico, and Raymond, "Enhancing Preschoolers' Self-Regulation Via Mindful Yoga," 374.

15. Deborah Bubela and Shanya Gaylord, "A Comparison of Preschoolers' Motor Abilities Before and After a 6 Week Yoga Program," *Yoga and Physical Therapy* 4, no. 2 (2014): 3.

16. Ibid.

17. Butzer et al., "School-Based Yoga Programs in the United States," 19.

18. Birdee et al., "Clinical Applications of Yoga for the Pediatric Population," 218.

19. Centers for Disease Control and Prevention, "Childhood Obesity Facts," www.cdc.gov/obesity/data/childhood.html.

20. Lisa Guernsey, "How True Are Our Assumptions about Screen Time?," National Association for the Education of Young Children, https://families.naeyc.org/learning-and-development/music-math-more/how-true-are-our-assumptions-about-screen-time.

Chapter Two

Yoga, Movement, and Early Learning

lthough some libraries are beginning to experiment with the incorporation of yoga into their storytime programs,[1] to date no research has been done on the benefits of yoga storytime nor are there any published outcomes assessments of this type of programming. Considering the limited size and scope of research into yoga and other contemplative practices for preschool children in general, this lack of specific information is hardly surprising. We can use what we know, however, about yoga and child development to draw some conclusions about how yoga may function as a tool to help young children learn.

Movement

It may be difficult for us to remember as adults, but for young children, movement is a learning process that requires intense concentration. During the early years of life, children are building the neural pathways that will shape how they think, how they learn, and even how they view the world. All of a child's early physical and sensory experiences are helping to build those pathways.[2]

In the early years of life, movement is among the brain's top priorities. Eventually, many movements will become *automated,* meaning that a child can do them without having to think about them. Before movement is automated, however, it overrides all other thinking activity. Put quite simply, "learning begins with the body."[3]

Yoga provides children an opportunity to practice and experience many movements, both common and novel, that can help them develop balance, body and spatial awareness, strength and stamina, flexibility, coordination, and control.

Through repeated experience of these basic elements of movement, moving the body becomes an automated process. This automation, which is developed over time and with practice, allows the child to now engage in other behaviors (such as talking, thinking, listening, etc.) simultaneously with body movement. Box 2.1 presents more information about movement and the process of automation.

The brain is made up of two hemispheres—the left and the right. The right side of the brain controls the left side of the body and vice versa. For the two halves of the brain to be able to communicate, neural pathways must be formed across the corpus callosum, or the midline of the brain. Cross-lateral movements—movements in which the arms and legs cross over the midline of the body—help to build these neural pathways that facilitate the communication between the two sides of the brain. This development is critical for early learning. As Connell and McCarthy explain:

> [W]hen children are just learning to write, they may reverse letters, such as transposing a *b* for a *d*. Adults might see this as a difficulty with writing, when in fact, it may simply mean that the child is still working to sort out his midlines. After all, the only difference between a *b* and a *d* is which side of the line the loop falls on. If a child hasn't mastered the sides of his own body, the brain simply isn't ready yet to translate the concept of "sides" to other things.[4]

Many yoga poses, such as twists, engage the body in cross-lateral movements. Cross-lateral movements activate both hemispheres and all four lobes of the brain and help the corpus callosum to develop more fully, heightening a child's cognitive functioning and increasing the child's ease of learning.[5]

Yoga provides children the opportunity to move in many ways, including cross-laterally, as they use their bodies to act out stories, express emotions, and move creatively. By including yoga and other forms of movement in our storytime programs, we are helping children automate their movement or learn how to move in a variety of ways without having to think about it. This automatic movement makes the brain more efficient, allowing children to focus more of their energy on

BOX 2.1

Movement and Automation

In *A Moving Child Is a Learning Child: How the Body Teaches the Brain to Think*, authors Gill Connell and Cheryl McCarthy explain that the brain can focus on only one conscious task at a time. It is only after a process has become automated that another task can be layered on top of it. This is what we as adults generally think of as multitasking, or doing more than one action at a time, such as walking and talking. When movement is being learned, it requires the full force of a child's cognitive energy. Once movement is automated, the child has more cognitive energy available for learning new things.

BOX 2.2

CASEL Social-Emotional Learning (SEL) Competencies

The Collaborative for Academic, Social, and Emotional Learning (CASEL) has identified the following five social-emotional learning (SEL) competencies that are critical to children's school and life success:

- *Self-awareness:* The ability to accurately recognize one's emotions and thoughts and their influence on behavior
- *Self-management:* The ability to regulate one's emotions, thoughts, and behaviors effectively in different situations
- *Social awareness:* The ability to take the perspective of and empathize with others from diverse backgrounds and cultures, to understand social and ethical norms for behavior, and to recognize family, school, and community resources and supports
- *Relationship skills:* The ability to establish and maintain healthy and rewarding relationships with diverse individuals and groups
- *Responsible decision making:* The ability to make constructive and respectful choices about personal behavior and social interactions based on consideration of ethical standards, safety concerns, social norms, the realistic evaluation of consequences of various actions, and the well-being of self and others

For more information about CASEL and social-emotional learning in children, visit www.casel.org.

learning the other things (such as letters and numbers) that they will need in order to become school ready.

Engaging in regular physical activity is also important for young children's overall health and well-being. The National Association for Sport and Physical Education (NASPE) recommends that preschoolers ages three to five spend at least sixty minutes per day engaged in structured physical activity, with additional time spent in unstructured physical activity. NASPE also recommends that adults responsible for the well-being of preschool-age children understand the importance of physical activity and "facilitate the child's movement skills."[6]

Social-Emotional Learning

The Collaborative for Academic, Social, and Emotional Learning (CASEL) defines social-emotional learning (SEL) as

the process through which children and adults acquire and effectively apply the knowledge, attitudes, and skills necessary to understand and manage emotions, set and achieve positive goals, feel and show empathy for others, establish and maintain positive relationships, and make responsible decisions.[7]

In 2015, CASEL recognized several school-based yoga and mindfulness programs in its *Guide: Effective Social and Emotional Learning Programs*.[8] Research has found that these programs can help students improve mood, reduce stress and tension, and regulate their emotions. Box 2.2 presents a list of social-emotional learning competencies as described by CASEL.

Yoga can support the development of SEL competencies in many ways. Improved body awareness can help children learn to recognize the physical sensations that accompany their feelings and emotions, supporting the development of self-awareness. Relaxation practices can help children learn to handle their feelings (e.g., to calm themselves when they feel upset), supporting the development of self-management. Moving the body in a noncompetitive way in a shared space with others can help children become more aware and considerate of others,[9] supporting the development of social awareness and relationship skills. Having the opportunity to take reasonable risks as they learn new yoga poses (e.g., when to take their hands off the supporting wall when learning a balance pose) provides the opportunity to practice responsible decision making.

The traditional principles of yoga, known in Sanskrit as the *yamas* and *niyamas,* can be incorporated into programs in a secular way, providing an opportunity for more explicit acknowledgment of SEL concepts. These yoga principles (as defined for children) include nonviolence (*ahimsa*), honesty (*satya*), generosity (*asteya*), moderation (*brahmacharya*), gratitude (*aparigraha*), cleanliness (*saucha*), contentment (*santosha*), hard work (*tapas*), self-knowledge (*svadhyaya*), and connection with the world outside oneself (*ishvara pranidhana*).[10] The correlation between these principles and the skills often recognized as important to children's social-emotional development is striking. There are many natural ways to incorporate these principles into the storytime setting.

The physical practice of yoga poses itself provides an opportunity to explore yoga principles and the SEL competencies they relate to. For example, learning a new yoga pose requires hard work, one of the yoga *niyamas*. Working hard to achieve a goal, such as the ability to form and hold a yoga pose, requires self-management, an SEL competency. Other examples include being peaceful to oneself by not forcing the body to do something it isn't ready to do (self-awareness) and connecting with others through the practice of group poses (relationship skills).

Explicit book selection is another way to incorporate SEL components into a yoga storytime. Research shows that even as young children are still developing their full range of emotions and their ability to identify and understand the emotions of others, they can recognize and respond to emotions in picture books.[11] Books can be selected that provide children with opportunities to explore their own feelings and the feelings of others. This recognition of emotions is the beginning step to developing empathy,[12] an important part of a child's social-emotional development.

BOX 2.3

Dialogic Reading, Movement, and Social-Emotional Learning

Dialogic reading is a technique in which the person reading the story aloud in a small-group setting asks strategic questions that bring the listener more deeply into the meaning of the story.[13] Let's use *The Feelings Book* by Todd Parr as an example to explore what dialogic reading that is intended to address the SEL skill of identifying one's feelings (part of self-awareness) might look like in the storytime setting. As the storytime leader, you could read the book aloud, asking questions such as the following:

- What does the word *cranky* mean? How do you know the person in this picture feels "cranky"?
- When was a time that you felt scared?
- What does it mean to "feel like a king"?

Provide children with time to think about and answer these questions either within the group setting or one-on-one with their adult caregivers. Follow up by asking more open-ended questions based on children's responses. Give a signal to acknowledge the end of the discussion before continuing to read aloud.

After reading the book, you could transition into a related movement activity. In this example, the specific SEL skill being practiced is identifying feelings. To continue exploring this skill through yoga and movement, play an instrumental song and allow the children to dance freely. Periodically, pause the music and call out a feeling or emotion. While the music is paused, the children freeze in a position that uses their bodies to express that specific feeling or emotion. Then invite the kids to move their bodies into a yoga pose that might feel good when they are experiencing this emotion or feeling. Once the music resumes, the children may continue dancing, and so on.

Dialogic reading can enhance a child's understanding of social-emotional concepts presented in some picture books. Box 2.3 explores the use of dialogic reading and movement to support children's SEL development in the storytime setting.

Early Literacy

Thanks largely to the accessibility of the Every Child Ready to Read (ECRR) initiative, today *early literacy* is a ubiquitous term among children's librarians. Storytimes are intentionally designed with the principles of early literacy development in mind. Ample opportunities are provided throughout the storytime to engage in the five early literacy practices recommended by ECRR (talk, sing, read, write, and play)[14] and to model for parents simple techniques they can use to continue this learning at home as their child's first teacher. Librarians have a wealth of tools at

Early Literacy and Movement— Results from a Recent Study

BOX 2.4

A 2015 study demonstrates a significant benefit to pairing movement with early literacy practices. The study of over four hundred children compared the early literacy development of children who received both early literacy instruction and a movement-based literacy activity with that of children who received only one of the two interventions. The early literacy intervention received was Let's Decode, a specific approach to teaching phonological awareness and decoding. The movement intervention, Moving On with Literacy, was a compilation of thirty action songs that the groups sang together while engaging in various movements which involved fine motor skill practice, eye-tracking, balance, rhythm, cross-lateral movement, gross motor skills, core strength, and aerobic capacity. Researchers found that children who received the early literacy and movement interventions together performed better than controls on assessments of literacy measures. This difference existed only for the children who received both the literacy and movement instruction, not the literacy or movement instruction only. These results indicate that teaching early literacy concepts and movement in tandem may be more beneficial for children's early literacy skill development than teaching early literacy concepts alone.

Source: Deborah Callcott, Lorraine Hammond, and Susan Hill, "The Synergistic Effect of Teaching a Combined Explicit Movement and Phonological Awareness Program to Preschool Aged Students," *Early Childhood Education Journal* 43, no. 3 (2015): 201–211.

their disposal that they use to deliver these early literacy–focused storytime programs, including books, recorded music, traditional rhymes and songs, flannelboard stories, puppets, digital media, and more. Yoga can serve as another tool that helps engage children and caregivers in early literacy practices. Box 2.4 summarizes the findings of a recent study which indicates that combining early literacy instruction with movement may be more effective than early literacy instruction alone.

All the elements of an early literacy–focused storytime will be present in a yoga storytime; the only difference is that these elements may be enhanced with movement. Welcome songs and rhymes may include simple movements that help warm up the body and prepare children for the bigger movements that will come later. As stories are told and books are read aloud, children may be encouraged to experiment with corresponding yoga poses. Recorded songs may be shared that encourage yoga-specific movements and shapes, such as a Sun Salutation song. All the early literacy practices are still present in the program, but a specific intention has been made to involve the body in the experience.

Embodied Play

Throughout this book I frequently describe yoga for children as *embodied play*. This term is meant to express that yoga can be used creatively to provide children with opportunities to use their bodies to explore themselves, their imaginations, their connections with others, and the world around them. Though sharing yoga with children does require some replication in order to learn the poses, more focus should be placed on encouraging children to use the movements and poses imaginatively.

From its beginning days, play has been an important part of teaching yoga to children in the West.[15] Children's yoga acknowledges and honors that young children learn through play; any yoga brought into the storytime setting should acknowledge and honor this fact as well. As children learn various animal poses, they can pretend to be those animals, hopping and ribbiting in Frog Pose, or barking and wagging their tails while in Dog Pose. As you share stories and songs, children are invited to play along, acting out the various scenes. They can use their bodies to concretely express abstract ideas, such as emotions. They can also work together cooperatively to solve problems, such as by using their bodies to create letters or shapes in small groups. All this is embodied play that allows children to explore physical movement, SEL skills, and early literacy practices for themselves, rather than simply replicating an instructed pose.

Bringing It All Together

By looking at some of the simple activities that we may use with children in an ocean- or fish-themed yoga storytime, we can begin to see how movement, social-emotional learning, and early literacy practices work together to stimulate the learning of the whole child.

In storytime, with the group standing together in a circle, encourage children to swim like fish within the pretend ocean at the middle of the circle, while listening to the sound of ocean waves, an upbeat instrumental song, or an action song about ocean animals, such as "I'm a Little Fish" by Laura Doherty. When moving together in a shared space, children must be aware of others and adjust their own behaviors accordingly. Children must take care not to bump into or step on the other "fish" swimming around them. This activity requires consideration and cooperation, skills that align with CASEL's relationship skills SEL competency.

Yoga is inherently noncompetitive. As a result, it provides the opportunity for children to accept the similarities and differences that exist between themselves and others. After the children have been swimming freely in the ocean for a bit, invite them to find their own space in the circle to practice Fish Pose. While you demonstrate your expression of this pose, there will inevitably be variances in the pose expression among the children and adult caregivers in the group. This can be a wonderful time to encourage an appreciation of this diversity, another skill that supports the relationship skills SEL competency. You might say, "Look at all the different kinds of fish we have in our ocean today! How beautiful!" As long as each individual child is in a shape that is comfortable for his body and is allowing him to express his version of a fish, no adjustments or comparisons need be made. Each individual shape can be celebrated, as children practice moving their own unique bodies in a novel way.

Practicing Fish Pose can provide an excellent opportunity to talk about vocabulary as well. Ask children to call out the names of the fish that they are today. If you've previously read a book that features lots of different kinds of fish, such as *Hooray for Fish!* by Lucy Cousins, refer to those vocabulary words. Tie in letter knowledge by asking the group to share the names of fish that start with *t* or *m* or any other letter you want to practice. Before you leave your ocean scene, allow children to use their bodies to express any other object that they might find in the ocean; it's perfectly fine for children to use their imaginations to rename a yoga pose they have previously learned, such as changing "Butterfly" Pose to "Clam" Pose. Provide an opportunity for children to share with their adult caregiver what ocean object they are. Encourage caregivers to ask open-ended, follow-up questions. After a few minutes, ring a bell to signal the end of this activity and the transition into your next storytime component.

Throughout this example, we can see how yoga and the movement inspired by yoga poses can engage children in body (swimming, making fish shapes), heart (cooperating, appreciating the diversity of others), and mind (creatively expressing an abstract idea, practicing vocabulary, and practicing letter knowledge).

Concluding Thoughts

Like books, music, and storytelling, yoga and movement are tools that librarians can use in their storytimes to support the early learning of young children. By having the opportunity to move their bodies, children further automate the process of moving in various ways, over time freeing their brains to focus on other kinds of learning. Through intentional book and activity selections, children can develop skills critical to their social-emotional learning. Movement can accompany, and even enhance, many of the early literacy–building practices encouraged by the Every Child Ready to Read initiative. Yoga allows children to engage in embodied play; it is a tool that enables them to use their bodies to creatively explore themselves and their world. With some learning, practice, and thoughtfulness, yoga can be a natural addition to storytime, enhancing and supporting what librarians are already doing daily.

NOTES

1. Stephanie C. Prato and Kristen Hanmer, "Promote Learning with a Yoga Storytime," *ALSC Blog,* Association for Library Service to Children (June 22, 2016), www.alsc.ala .org/blog/2016/06/yoga-storytime/.

2. Gill Connell and Cheryl McCarthy, *A Moving Child Is a Learning Child: How the Body Teaches the Brain to Think* (Minneapolis, MN: Free Spirit Publishing, 2014), 7.

3. Ibid., 6.

4. Ibid., 114.

5. Carla Hannaford, *Smart Moves: Why Learning Is Not All in Your Head* (Arlington, VA: Great Ocean Publishers, 1995): 81, quoted in Rae Pica, "Beyond Physical Development: Why Young Children Need to Move," *Young Children* 52, no. 6 (1997): 10.

6. National Association for Sport and Physical Education (NASPE), "Active Start— Physical Activity Guidelines for Children Birth to Five Years," excerpted in National Association for the Education of Young Children, "Nutrition and Physical Fitness," *Beyond the Journal* (2006), http://journal.naeyc.org/btj/200605/NASPEGuidelines BTJ.pdf.

7. Collaborative for Academic, Social, and Emotional Learning (CASEL), "What Is SEL?," www.casel.org/what-is-sel.

8. Collaborative for Academic, Social, and Emotional Learning (CASEL), *2015 CASEL Guide: Effective Social and Emotional Learning Programs,* http://secondaryguide.casel .org/mindfulness-program-descriptions.html.

9. Rae Pica, "Beyond Physical Development: Why Young Children Need to Move," *Young Children* 52, no. 6 (1997): 5.

10. Lisa Flynn, *Yoga for Children: 200+ Yoga Poses, Breathing Exercises, and Meditations for Healthier, Happier, More Resilient Children* (Avon, MA: Adams Media, 2013), 47–53.

11. Maria Nikolajeva, "Picturebooks and Emotional Literacy," *Reading Teacher* 67, no. 4 (2013): 250.

12. Ibid., 251.

13. Brooke Graham Doyle and Wendie Bramwell, "Promoting Emergent Literacy and Social-Emotional Learning through Dialogic Reading," *Reading Teacher* 59, no. 6 (2006): 555.

14. Lynn Neary, "Talk, Sing, Read, Write, Play: How Libraries Reach Kids Before They Can Read," National Public Radio (December 30, 2014), www.npr.org/ 2014/12/30/373783189/talk-sing-read-write-play-how-libraries-reach-kids-before -they-can-read.

15. Marsha Wenig, *YogaKids: Educating the Whole Child through Yoga* (New York: Stewart, Tabori and Chang, 2003), 7.

Chapter Three

Yoga Storytime Fundamentals

A t this stage you may be beginning to see the potential that yoga storytime has to offer—its physical and early learning benefits for young children, its opportunities for sparking adult–child interaction, its potential for attracting families to your library. However, you may still be wondering about the details—how do I actually develop a yoga storytime program? This chapter will provide an in-depth explanation for how to set up and deliver your yoga storytime.

Yoga Storytime Program Design

At its heart, a yoga storytime is about encouraging embodied play. The design of a yoga storytime has much in common with the design of a traditional storytime program, but intentional choices are made to engage children physically and emotionally throughout the program. The level and amount of movement incorporated into a yoga storytime can vary from program to program and presenter to presenter. There is ample room for creativity, and presenters should make sure above all that they are enthusiastic and comfortable with what they are choosing to present. As anyone who works with children quickly learns, your own enjoyment of what you are doing greatly influences how fun and engaging your program is for your group. Authenticity is key.

In my yoga storytimes, I like to take the program through an energetic peak and wind-down period, and I select my activities and materials to accommodate this pattern. We begin with a song to welcome everyone to our group. Then we engage in a warm-up activity that gets the body moving and allows children an opportunity to practice listening and following directions. From here we move on to more energetic books and songs that inspire the exploration of yoga poses and bigger movements. Then we transition from energetic movement to a calmer experience. Children and their adult caregivers are invited to sit together, cuddle up if they'd like, and enjoy a listening story as a way to relax before we move into our final resting period. These final stories are not selected for movement components or even necessarily to correspond with the overall program theme; rather, they introduce a concept that directly addresses our connections to our inner selves, one another, and the world at large. Finally, it's time to rest briefly, typically one to three minutes. During this time, I usually turn out or dim the lights, encourage everyone to rest comfortably on their own or snuggled up with their grown-up, and play soft music or nature sounds to help aid children's relaxation. When it's time to get up, I gently ring a bell to signal the transition. Then we sing our goodbye song, and everyone is free to enjoy the remainder of their day. Box 3.1 offers a basic yoga storytime planning template based on this design.

As with a traditional storytime, a yoga storytime will typically last thirty to forty-five minutes. Presenters should incorporate the same components that they use in their other storytimes, including books, storytelling, music, rhymes, and digital tools. Within this template, presenters can include yoga poses and movement to the degree that they feel comfortable and that seems appropriate for the group. Be present and pay attention to what your group needs throughout the program. Be prepared to adjust as needed! If you are reading a story without movement and have completely lost the group's attention, switch gears and add in a movement song. If the group is looking tired and you have a big movement story planned, maybe lessen the amount of movement you planned to share in order to give them a chance to rest. Starting and ending the program with a standard opening and closing routine (such as a song that acknowledges each child by name) is encouraged; this routine can help signal to children what is happening.

Yoga classes the world over end with a brief period of relaxation, typically three to five minutes, known in Sanskrit as *savasana,* which translates in English to Corpse Pose. This is the time when the activity of the practice is completely let go and the objective is simply to rest quietly. Including a few minutes of relaxation for your group is a wonderful way to end your yoga storytime. Asking children to be quiet and still for a few moments can help them learn self-regulation. It also provides an opportunity for children and caregivers to take a break from the constant overstimulation that is so often a part of our lives in this digitally saturated era.

To make this rest period appropriate for preschool-age children, you will want to keep it nice and short, approximately thirty seconds to two minutes. Adults typically practice this pose lying on their backs, but it is perfectly fine to encourage children to rest in any way that they feel comfortable and capable of being still for a few moments. They may even want to use the time to cuddle up with their grown-up. You may want to play some calming music or nature sounds during this time to aid relaxation.

Let children know that they are not expected to sleep or nap during this time. As the storytime leader, you should lie down and take a brief rest along with the group,

Basic Yoga Storytime Planning Template

BOX 3.1

Ages: 3 to 6 years

Approximate time: 30 minutes

Theme: _____

Introduction and caregiver information

Welcome song or opening routine

Warm-up songs and rhymes

Opening movement or yoga book

Yoga or movement song

Storytelling or game

Yoga or movement song

Cool-down listening story

Rest

Good-bye song or closing routine

in order to reassure the children that they are not missing anything interesting. It is perfectly normal for some children to whisper, giggle, or fidget; don't try to control this. Ring a bell or chime or use some other cue to let the group know when it is time to transition out of rest back into the remainder of the closing routine.

Selecting Materials

Selecting materials for yoga storytime has much in common with the way materials are selected for any storytime program. The presenter will seek out books, songs, digital media, and the like that are age appropriate and fun to share with young children. This section will provide additional guidance for selecting materials for a yoga storytime that inspire the use of yoga and movement.

BOOKS

When selecting books, use the same criteria that you apply in all storytimes: Is the story interesting and engaging? Do the illustrations and physical design of the book present well to a group? Am I seeking out and including books by and about diverse groups of people? Can I use this book in a way that models participation in important early literacy practices? On top of these standard criteria, assess whether this book inspires opportunities for movement or the exploration of SEL concepts.

Books that include movement within the story are a natural fit for a yoga story-time. Sometimes, movement may serve as the central theme of the story, such as in *Stretch* by Doreen Cronin. Often, various movements (such as jumping, flying, swimming, etc.) will be paired with characters in the story (typically animals), such as in *My Friends* by Taro Gomi. When using books in a yoga storytime setting, you have many options for how and when to incorporate movement and how much movement to incorporate, including the following:

- Read the book and then, after reading, come back to a few select passages to act out.
- Read the book and act out the movements as they are described.
- Read the book, act out the movements as they are described, and add yoga poses inspired by the various characters.

Your individual style and the degree of movement you feel comfortable sharing will influence how you use the book.

Books with animal characters are particularly well suited for use in yoga story-

---

BOX 3.2

Recommended Books for Yoga Storytime

Animal Books

Balancing Act by Ellen Stoll Walsh

Butterfly, Butterfly by Petr Horáček

Counting Lions: Portraits from the Wild by Katie Cotton, illustrated by Stephen Walton

Dancing Feet! by Lindsay Craig, illustrated by Marc Brown

From Head to Toe by Eric Carle

I Can Help by David Hyde Costello

Jump! by Scott M. Fischer

Jump, Frog, Jump! by Robert Kalan, illustrated by Bob Barton

The Little Little Girl with the Big Big Voice by Kristen Balouch

Little White Rabbit by Kevin Henkes

Marta! Big and Small by Jen Arena, illustrated by Angela Dominguez

Mouse Was Mad by Linda Urban, illustrated by Henry Cole

Move! by Robin Page, illustrated by Steve Jenkins

My Friends by Taro Gomi

Over in the Meadow by Jane Cabrera

Pouch! by David Ezra Stein

Scoot! by Cathryn Falwell

Still a Gorilla! by Kim Norman, illustrated by Chad Geran

Swimmy by Leo Lionni

The Very Busy Spider by Eric Carle

Who Hops? by Katie Davis

Yoga Books

The ABCs of Yoga for Kids by Teresa Anne Power, illustrated by Kathleen Rietz

The Happiest Tree: A Yoga Story by Uma Krishmaswami, illustrated by Ruth Jeyaveeran

time because nearly every animal imaginable can be expressed physically through a yoga pose. The animal names given to the various poses shared in chapter 4 illustrate this characteristic. Some yoga poses have obvious animal-inspired origins, such as Downward-Facing Dog and Cobra Pose. Other poses can be transformed into animal shapes through the use of imagination, such as by renaming Crescent Moon Pose as Rhinoceros Pose, inspired by interpreting the clasped hands above the head as a rhinoceros's horn. The rhyme-based stories by Jane Cabrera (such as *Row, Row, Row Your Boat*) are particularly great examples of books that lend themselves to a natural incorporation of animal-inspired yoga poses.

Books that celebrate the natural world are also ideal for use in yoga storytime, such as *Call Me Tree / Llámame árbol* by Maya Christina Gonzalez. Many yoga

I Am Yoga by Susan Verde, illustrated by Peter H. Reynolds

Little Yoga: A Toddler's First Book of Yoga by Rebecca Whitford, illustrated by Martina Selway

A Morning with Grandpa by Sylvia Liu, illustrated by Christina Forshay

My Daddy Is a Pretzel: Yoga for Parents and Kids by Baron Baptise, illustrated by Sophie Fatus

Rachel's Day in the Garden: A Kids Yoga Spring Colors Book by Giselle Shardlow, illustrated by Hazel Quintanilla

Yoga for Kids: Simple Animals Poses for Any Age by Lorena V. Pajalunga, illustrated by Anna Forlati

The Yoga Game by Kathy Beliveau, illustrated by Farida Zaman

You Are a Lion! And Other Fun Yoga Poses by Taeeun Yoo

Listening Stories

All in a Day by Cynthia Rylant, illustrated by Nikki McClure

Breathe by Scott Magoon

Can You Say Peace? by Karen Katz

Gracias / Thanks by Pat Mora, illustrated by John Parra

I Know the River Loves Me / Yo sé que el río me ama by Maya Christina Gonzalez

I Love Our Earth by Bill Martin Jr. and Michael Sampson, photographs by Dan Lipow

I Wish You More by Amy Krouse Rosenthal, illustrated by Tom Lichtenheld

It's Tough to Lose Your Balloon by Jarrett J. Krosoczka

Little Monkey Calms Down by Michael Dahl, illustrated by Oriol Vidal

Peace by Wendy Anderson Halperin

The Peace Book by Todd Parr

Peace Is an Offering by Annette LeBox, illustrated by Stephanie Graegin

That's Love by Sam Williams, illustrated by Mique Moriuchi

Waiting by Kevin Henkes

What Does Peace Feel Like? by Vladimir Radunsky

Whoever You Are by Mem Fox, illustrated by Leslie Staub

poses are inspired by landforms, such as Mountain and Tree. As with animal poses, traditional names for yoga poses can be reimagined to physically express different elements of the natural world. Examples of these interpretations can be found in the pose descriptions in chapter 4, including the Waterfall, Star, and Moon variations of Standing Pose.

There is a small but growing genre of yoga-inspired picture books that tend to incorporate yoga poses directly into the stories themselves, such as *Rachel's Day in the Garden* by Giselle Shardlow. Shardlow has written a series of self-published, yoga-inspired picture books (of varying quality), including many that have been translated into languages other than English. Other yoga-inspired picture books, such as *The Yoga Game by the Sea* by Kathy Beliveau, offer riddles in which readers are encouraged to guess the yoga shape and then try it out for themselves. Though books that incorporate yoga so explicitly can be quite fun to share, you should not feel limited to using this type of book, nor should you sacrifice the other criteria you employ when selecting books for storytime.

Picture books that include messages related to yoga principles (see chapter 2), such as peace, respect for the environment, and care for one another, are good choices for listening stories that allow children to cool down from all the movement they've experienced throughout the program. These kinds of stories provide a natural transition from the activity of the program into the period of final relaxation. Books by Todd Parr (such as *The Peace Book*) are great examples of stories that can help children make this transition from movement to rest. See Box 3.2 for a list of recommended books for yoga storytime.

STORYTELLING

Storytelling is a natural way to incorporate yoga and movement into your storytime. You can do this by modifying picture book favorites into oral stories, such as *I Went Walking* by Sue Williams. In this example, act out the story by walking in place, giving an animal sound clue for the next creature, acting out its movements, then sharing a yoga pose inspired by that animal. Props such as a flannelboard or puppets are helpful tools for storytelling. The flannelboard is a particularly effective way to add a visual element to your storytelling and can be used to share stories based on picture books as well as folktales, songs, and rhymes.

Traditional stories and stories from picture books alike can be told aloud, with or without the use of props. Select stories using the same criteria that you use to select books for yoga storytime, looking for natural ways to incorporate yoga poses and movement throughout. You can even make up your own stories! For example, select a setting to "visit" (e.g., the beach), engage in the actions necessary to get to that place (e.g., walking, driving in a car, or flying in an airplane), make some yoga poses resembling the various things you see there (e.g., seaweed, clams, starfish, and boats), then engage in the actions to journey back to the storytime space.

Flannel Friday (http://flannelfridaystorytime.blogspot.com/), an online resource in which librarians share flannelboard patterns and stories each week via blog posts, is a wonderful place to find storytelling inspiration. *Storytime Yoga: Teaching Yoga to Children through Story* by Sydney Solis is a helpful resource for finding stories that have been adapted to include yoga poses and movement; it is also available in Spanish as *Yoga con cuentos: Cómo enseñar yoga a los niños mediante el uso de cuentos.* In addition to presenting numerous folktales that have been modified in this way, this resource offers guidance on how to select and adapt folktales and other stories into storytelling that involves the body. A number of video demonstrations of yoga stories and songs are available on the Storytime Yoga for Kids YouTube page as well (www.youtube.com/user/StorytimeYoga).

MUSIC AND RHYMES

Singing and rhyming are powerful tools for helping young children develop critical language and literacy skills; this is why songs and rhymes are staple components in nearly every storytime program. Rhyming and singing slow down language, aiding in the development of phonological awareness, or the ability to hear and manipulate the small sounds within words. They also expose children to a variety of words, important for the development of a robust vocabulary. Traditional songs, as well as original children's music, can be helpful tools for establishing the routine format of the program, providing movement opportunities and practicing yoga poses, making transitions, and cooling down.

Traditional children's songs and rhymes are likely to be known by the children attending your storytime. Children love having the chance to share a song or rhyme that they know. Some songs and rhymes may have movements that accompany the words, such as "Head, Shoulders, Knees, and Toes." This song is a great warm-up for the beginning of storytime to practice body part vocabulary and get the group moving in some small ways. Mix it up by singing the song at regular speed, then super slowly, then as fast as you can! Other traditional songs and rhymes can inspire yoga movements. For example, you can sing "Old MacDonald Had a Farm" and add yoga poses to go with the various farm animals, such as dog, cow, and horse. Add a flannelboard, puppets, or digital media tools to include a visual element. Lots of rhymes, traditional and more modern, can be modified to include both general and yoga-inspired movement. See the pose descriptions in chapter 4 and the program plans in chapter 5 for more guidance.

Today a wealth of children's musicians are creating active, engaging music for kids. Many of these songs include movement suggestions right in the lyrics and make great additions to a yoga storytime. Use these kinds of songs to get kids moving at the beginning of the program, to continue your selected theme after reading a book, or anytime that the group seems a little wiggly and ready for active movement. Some original children's songs may inspire the use of yoga poses to accompany the animals or objects named in the song. A number of talented children's musicians are creating yoga music—songs specifically created to teach and inspire children's yoga. For example, Kira Willey's "Dance for the Sun" guides children through a gentle Sun Salutation practice, and Bari Koral's "Butterfly" encourages children to move through various yoga poses as they act out the life cycle of a butterfly. See Box 3.3 for a list of recommended children's songs for yoga storytime.

BOX 3.3

Recommended Songs for Yoga Storytime

Movement Songs

"Clap Your Hands" from *Here Come the ABCs* (2006) by They Might Be Giants

"The Goldfish" from *The Best of the Laurie Berkner Band* (2010) by The Laurie Berkner Band

"Jump, Jump" from *I'm a Rock Star* (2010) by Joanie Leeds and the Nightlights

"Jump Up, Turn Around" from *Moving Rhymes for Modern Times* (2006) by Jim Gill

"Knuckles Knees" from *Jim Gill Sings Do Re Mi on His Toe Leg Knee* (1999) by Jim Gill

"Silly Dance Contest" from *Jim Gill Sings the Sneezing Song and Other Contagious Tunes* (1993) by Jim Gill

"Spaghetti Legs" from *Jim Gill Sings the Sneezing Song and Other Contagious Tunes* (1993) by Jim Gill

Songs That Inspire Yoga Poses

"I'm a Little Fish" from *In a Heartbeat* (2014) by Laura Doherty

"Rockin' at the Zoo" from *Kids in the City* (2009) by Laura Doherty

"Say Hi to the Animals" from *Happy Lemons* (2015) by Ralph's World

Yoga-Specific Songs

"Apple Tree" from *The Apple Tree and the Honey Bee* (2014) by Bari Koral Family Rock Band

"Back to the Farm" from *The Apple Tree and the Honey Bee* (2014) by Bari Koral Family Rock Band

"Butterfly" from *Anna and the Cupcakes* (2012) by Bari Koral Family Rock Band

"Dance for the Sun" from *Dance for the Sun: Yoga Songs for Kids* (2006) by Kira Willey

"That's What They Do" from *Come Play Yoga!* (2008) by Karma Kids Yoga

"Yoga Clock" from *Come Play Yoga!* (2008) by Karma Kids Yoga

Resting Songs

"Be Still" from *Breathe In: Children's Songs for Mindfulness and Awareness* (2015) by Lianne Bassin

"Colors" from *Dance for the Sun: Yoga Songs for Kids* (2006) by Kira Willey

"We Are One" from *It's a Big World* (2007) by Renee and Jeremy

DIGITAL TOOLS

Today it is easier than ever to find new ideas to incorporate into storytime settings thanks to the digital tools and resources that are available online and through mobile applications. This section will highlight a few digital tools that I have found especially helpful for yoga storytime.

- *YouTube*. Librarians from all across the country are using YouTube today to showcase the many resources their libraries have to offer, including storytime. Many libraries have YouTube channels dedicated to sharing songs, rhymes, and early literacy tips with the families they serve and the world at large. See Box 3.4 for a list of recommended library YouTube channels. The box also includes two recommended kids' yoga YouTube channels that will be useful to anyone leading a yoga storytime.

- *Apps*. At the time of writing, I could not locate any apps specific to children's yoga that I felt were strong enough to recommend in this book. However, you are certainly encouraged to explore this on your own. Little eLit (https://littleelit.com) is a fantastic online resource for anyone interested in learning more about the use of apps in storytime. It is possible that some of the apps already explored and reviewed on this site for general storytimes would also be useful in yoga storytimes. I have found the following two free apps to be helpful tools for yoga storytime.

  Insight Timer—https://insighttimer.com

  Insight Timer is a free meditation time application available for Android and iOS devices. It is a simple timer that offers multiple chime and bell sounds. It is useful when you are engaging in a timed activity and want to use a sound to alert the group that it is time to transition to another part of the program. The most obvious way to use this timer is to signal the end of the rest period; this application will allow you to lie down and rest with the group rather than watch the clock. Having everyone in the group lying down in rest together often encourages children who may be reluctant to rest to go ahead and give it a try. This application also has an extensive guided meditation section that includes many instrumental songs for yoga and meditation which would be nice to play during the resting period. You can also explore the guided meditations to find tools for yourself that allow you to center and relax before leading the yoga storytime program.

  White Noise—www.tmsoft.com/white-noise

  White Noise is a sounds application available on multiple platforms. The free version offers dozens of sounds, including many sounds from the natural environment. These sounds can be fun to incorporate into yoga storytime during periods of storytelling or rest. For example, you could play the "Beach Waves Crashing" sound while pretending to visit the beach or play the "Frogs" sound during rest at the end of a frog-themed program.

BOX 3.4

Recommended YouTube Channels

Brooklyn Public Library—www.youtube.com/user/BPLvideos
"Children's Videos" playlist presents dozens of video demonstrations of songs and rhymes, as well as early literacy information, in multiple languages.

Colorado State Library—www.youtube.com/user/coloradolibraries
"StoryBlocks" playlist presents more than fifty video demonstrations of songs and rhymes in multiple languages.

Jbrary—www.youtube.com/user/Jbrary
Two librarians offer an extensive collection of song and rhyme demonstrations.

Johnson County Library—www.youtube.com/user/jocolibrary
Look for the "6 by 6 Finger Play and Wordless Books" playlist for over one hundred video demonstrations.

King County Library System—www.youtube.com/user/kingcountylibrary
Look for "Tell Me a Story" playlists for hundreds of demonstrations of songs and rhymes in multiple languages.

Washington County Cooperative Library System—www.youtube.com/user/Birth2Six
A vast collection of English and Spanish storytime songs and rhymes, demonstrated by library staff.

Bari Koral—www.youtube.com/user/barikoral
Bari Koral is a musician who has released four children's albums. Many of her songs have yoga themes and include yoga poses and movements in the lyrics. On her YouTube channel, several high-quality music videos accompany such songs and show real children moving through the various yoga poses as they sing along. For librarians using an interactive whiteboard, projector, or other such technology, playing these videos as you sing and move along with the songs is a fun way to share with families a free resource that they can access on their own at home.

Cosmic Kids Yoga—www.youtube.com/user/CosmicKidsYoga
Cosmic Kids Yoga is an online children's yoga program created by a children's yoga teacher from England known as Jaime. The themed shows use storytelling to teach and explore yoga in a child-friendly way. Viewing a few of these programs would be useful for anyone leading a yoga storytime who is interested in learning more about what yoga for kids looks like in action and how to include storytelling in programs. Of particular interest is the playlist titled "Learn All the Kids Yoga Postures!"—http://tinyurl.com/zvs7m89. These brief videos (typically less than thirty seconds) show the host teaching a yoga pose for a child audience. These videos are a great resource for anyone who wants to learn some new child-friendly yoga poses and would be fun to incorporate into the yoga storytime setting via an interactive whiteboard or projector. Again, this program exposes families to a free resource that they can use on their own at home.

- *Music Streaming Services.* Rather than investing in multiple CDs for a story-time reference collection, libraries not already using a music streaming service such as Google Play, Amazon Music, Apple Music, Spotify, and the like may want to consider doing so. Typically these services charge a monthly fee for access to their entire library of music, which can be accessed via a mobile application with a data or Internet connection. This generally works out to be much less expensive than purchasing multiple CDs, though CDs should certainly still be purchased for the circulating music collection for families to use at home. These streaming services often allow users to create their own music playlists for easy reference, which is often much less cumbersome to use in the storytime setting than having to switch between multiple CDs, locate tracks, and so on. Some services also allow users to download a certain amount of music for offline listening when an Internet connection is not available.

Yoga Storytime Planning Logistics

Now that we've walked through basic yoga storytime design and the selection of books, music, and other materials, let's clarify some of the logistical details around planning and implementing a yoga storytime program. A case study of how one library is using yoga in programming for children can be found in Box 3.5.

AGES

A yoga storytime should target children who are old enough to engage in the yoga poses and movement components that your storytime will be exploring. An ideal target age for a yoga storytime is three to six years old. Adult caregivers should attend the storytime with their child and be encouraged to participate at their comfort level. See Box 3.6 for guidance on setting expectations and behavior standards for adults.

REGISTRATION

There are advantages and drawbacks to requiring registration for any storytime program. Because a yoga storytime is very active and requires more space for movement than other programs, it may be helpful to require program registration in order to limit the size of the group to a number that feels workable to you. If your program is set up as a limited series that requires registration (e.g., four or six weeks) rather than an ongoing program, you have the advantage of being able to introduce yoga poses and movement components (such as a Sun Salutation, for example) that children can learn and build on from week to week. However, the downside is that requiring advance registration for a program can create a barrier to attendance for families who would be more apt to join if they could simply drop in when convenient for them.

PHYSICAL SETUP

Set up your program in a room that is large enough to allow adults and children

BOX 3.5

Yoga Play! at Akron-Summit County (Ohio) Public Library

Sophia Louise Van Der Schyf and Anne-Marie Savoie are two passionate, high-energy, and dedicated children's librarians who work together to create a series of multisensory exploration programs for preschoolers that they call Yoga Play! Their programs use songs, storytelling, and books to introduce children to movement and yoga poses. They also incorporate breathing practices and dialogic reading to help children learn self-regulation strategies and discuss social-emotional learning concepts. Each program concludes with a period of free play, in which children and caregivers explore themed discovery centers that provide opportunities for children to engage their imaginations while developing early learning skills. The result is a truly larger-than-life journey in which children are completely engaged in body, heart, and mind.

Sophia Louise and Anne-Marie first began to make the connection between yoga and storytime when they decided to participate in a children's yoga training offered in their area. Though they paid for the training mostly on their own with minimal financial support from their library, the library was able to support them by allowing them to take the training on work time. Throughout the training, the librarians realized more and more how much yoga for preschool children and library storytime have in common. They saw how naturally yoga and storytime could work together to honor the curiosity of young children and simultaneously support their physical development and early learning. "We were seeing how we could use yoga as

a platform," Sophia Louise recalls, "to encourage imagination, curiosity, and play." After participating in the training, Anne-Marie and Sophia Louise began to notice children's yoga programs cropping up in all kinds of nontraditional spaces in Akron, such as museums and parks. The two wanted to use their new skills to seize upon this growing enthusiasm. Sophia Louise explains, "It's critical to continually be scanning the community for new interests and responding to them in order for the library to remain relevant and exciting." Anne-Marie adds that they knew their ideas for this program could help bust some of the stereotypes and misconceptions about the library. "This program doesn't ask kids to just sit still and listen to stories. Yes, it's about reading, but it's also about fun and play! We want to make it clear that this isn't your grandpa's library!" They pitched their ideas to their manager, who was supportive, and Yoga Play! was born.

In August 2016, I had the opportunity to observe a session of Yoga Play! The theme was space, and it was truly an out-of-this-world voyage. The environment was designed to stimulate the imagination as soon as children entered the room. A recycled space mural created on a large sheet of black butcher paper by children in another program was repurposed as a backdrop that stretched around the circle in which the group was sitting. As the children settled in, Sophia Louise and Anne-Marie took turns moving through the various components of the storytime portion of the program, singing the group welcome song, connecting with the breath, and warming up with some simple space-themed movement rhymes. As they introduced the space theme, there was a wonderful group discussion about space and the solar system. Children practiced breathing with long exhales by blowing a small star attached to a long strip of laminate, which they were then able to add to the space mural. They read *Zoom! Zoom! Zoom! I'm Off to the Moon!* by Dan Yaccarino, a rhyming book about a space journey. Then it was time for some storytelling with yoga poses inspired by a yoga story found on the DVD *Once Upon a Mat* by Namaste Kid. The children moved through Extended Side Angle, Crescent Moon, Star, and Extended Mountain Poses. Then the energy began to calm down, with some more gentle breathing and a rest period accompanied by the sounds of space. This concluded the yoga storytime portion of the program, and when the children transitioned out of their rest, the room divider was lifted, revealing multiple space-themed discovery centers and crafts that the children were now free to explore with their grown-ups. The discovery centers included a rocket ship, a control center, a shooting star craft, and a group space collage in which the children used precut shapes to add their own astronauts, rockets, planets, and the like. These discovery center props are truly spectacular and can be seen at www.pinterest.com/akronlibrary/childrens-library-yoga-play. They are created from mostly recycled materials, and many (such as the rocket ship) have been repurposed and used in various programs over and over again for years. Devon Brinkman has been bringing her three children (a five-year-

old and four-year-old twins) to the Yoga Play! sessions since they began last year, and she raves about how her children have engaged in more imaginative play at home and how the whole family uses the breathing practices in their daily routine.

Overall, each Yoga Play! session lasts about an hour. Sophia Louise and Anne-Marie design and present the programs in tandem. They had no idea what the initial reception would be, so they decided to offer their first series as a pilot to test the waters. Now they regularly offer Yoga Play! once a quarter as a four-week series. They do not require advance registration, and they serve about ten families per program on average. Anne-Marie and Sophia Louise are interested in taking a scaled-down version of the program out into the community to children who are not able to visit the library. Though neither describes herself as a "yogi," they have received basic training in teaching yoga to children and feel comfortable exploring movement, yoga poses, and simple breathing practices in the storytime setting. Though their exceptionally creative discovery center props may be more elaborate than what other librarians are able to offer, both Sophia Louise and Anne-Marie are quick to say that a yoga storytime program does not have to be anything fancy. They hope that their specific style may inspire others to consider active and hands-on programming for preschoolers that is intentionally designed to engage children physically, to provide them with opportunities to connect with their inner selves and the world around them, and to stimulate their imaginations through creative play.

to sit together in a circle on the floor so that everyone can see you. Be sure that there is enough room for the group to move through the various poses and creative movement components that you have planned for your program. Ensure that the floor is clean, so that participants will feel comfortable sitting and moving on it. Though adults are encouraged to sit with and participate with their child, some adults may have a difficult time sitting on the floor for a sustained period, so have chairs available for those who need them. The room should be as free as possible of distractions that may grab the attention of young children. Have a chair or cart for your own supplies (books, flannelboard, chime, etc.) that keeps them out of the reach of young children.

BOX 3.6

Setting Expectations and Behavior Standards for Parents and Caregivers

It's helpful to spend a few minutes explaining some clear participation guidelines for parents at the beginning of your program.

Encourage adults to participate at the level that is appropriate for them today. When children see their parents and caregivers participating in the program, they often feel more comfortable participating as well. However, not everything that is done in a yoga storytime will be a good choice for every adult body in the room, so adults must make good decisions for themselves regarding what physical activity is or is not appropriate for them. This is particularly important when the person leading the yoga storytime is not a trained yoga teacher. Adults should know they can skip any of the movement activities that they wish.

Remind adults that they are modeling yoga for children, and encourage them to make preschool-appropriate choices with their yoga poses. An adult with a regular yoga practice may be very comfortable bringing one leg into half lotus while practicing Tree Pose. However, this shape is not appropriate for a group of preschool children because it requires a level of balance they have probably not yet developed. It would be more appropriate for the adult in this situation to choose a less demanding version of Tree, perhaps standing near a wall to help with balance, with one foot resting lower on the leg, such as at the ankle or calf. This practice models a much more age-appropriate version of the pose.

Remind adults that what happens in a yoga storytime is very different from what happens in an adult yoga class. Yoga storytime is designed to be developmentally appropriate for young children—therefore, we use stories, songs, and play to inspire our movement. A yoga pose that adults may recognize (Balasana, or Child's Pose, for example) might have many different names depending on how it

SUPPLIES

A very common yoga prop used with students of all ages, and which may be useful in your yoga storytime as well, is a chime. Another instrument, such as a drum or a tambourine, could be substituted and used in a similar way. As you sing a welcoming song, pass the instrument around the group to provide each child an opportunity to share his name and make his own sound. Use the instrument as a cue to bring the group back to stillness and quiet when the children become very active and excited. You can also use the instrument or chime to cue a return to wakefulness after a period of rest at the end of the program. Many types of chimes and instruments are available; select something inexpensive that is easy for young children to manipulate and that you can replace if it is broken or damaged.

is used in a story or movement activity (such as Egg, Seed, Oval, or Rock).

Remind adults that children explore yoga in different ways depending on their age, mood, personality, and other factors. Some children will be excited to dive right into the yoga poses and movement components of your program. Some may need to hang back and watch for a while. Some may find a shape that they really enjoy and want to make again and again while the rest of the group moves on to other shapes. Some may make shapes that look different from what you, the storytime presenter, are demonstrating. All these responses are fine. Sharing yoga with children provides them with the opportunity to explore movement within their own bodies; explicitly remind parents that they should not feel any pressure to monitor or adjust the shapes their child makes. As long as the children are moving in a safe way, they should be encouraged to explore the movement independently. This exploration itself is much more important than making a shape that looks precisely like the shape being modeled.

Offer any specific behavior guidelines that you would like adults to help you enforce. Although it's important to encourage adults to be "hands-off" in terms of adjusting their child's body or forcing participation, it's also important to let adults know specifically what you do expect them to help you with in terms of behavior. For example, you may ask the adults to help you keep the group in the circle configuration so children are not coming into the middle of the circle or up to you as the presenter unless such movement is included in a specific part of the program. You may need to inform the group of the library's policy regarding posting photos of children's programs on social media. You may want to remind adults to silence their cell phones. Think through the behavior guidelines that are critical for your program to work and share those with adults as specifically as possible so they know clearly what they can allow their children to explore on their own and when they need to step in to keep the program enjoyable for everyone in the group.

Yoga mats are not necessary for a yoga storytime, though it is up to you and your library to decide whether you would like to invest in a supply of yoga mats for your program or encourage families to bring their own. If the floor of the area where you are offering your program is uncarpeted, or if you are presenting your program outside, consider asking families to bring mats or towels to sit on, or consider providing mats. Large rolls of yoga mat can be purchased and cut to custom sizes; for libraries that choose to provide mats, this option may be more cost-effective than purchasing many individual mats. Regular-sized yoga mats can be cut in half to make smaller yoga mat squares that are an appropriate size for young children. If you do choose to provide mats or allow families to supply their own, be aware that mats can be a tripping hazard for young children. Move the mats out of the way any time you are playing games or using songs that encourage free-form running, jumping, dancing, and so on.

Supplies typically available in a yoga studio setting (bolsters, blankets, blocks, etc.) can be used in a variety of ways in a yoga storytime but are not necessary. Likewise, supplies often used in library children's programs (parachutes, bubbles, art supplies, etc.) can be incorporated in nearly endless ways into a yoga storytime, though a simple setup with minimal extras can also work just fine.

PROMOTING YOUR PROGRAM

A yoga storytime is a different kind of program, and you may find that it helps you attract a different audience to your library. How you promote your program will, of course, factor into this difference. Some specific considerations include the following:

- *Naming your program.* Whether to use the word *yoga* in your program description will depend on many variables, including the cultures and values of your local community and your library organization. In many areas, using *yoga* in your program name will be well received and may capture the attention of families looking for a healthy activity they can do with their young children. In other areas, there may be some pushback against offering anything with *yoga* in the name in the library setting. Remember, yoga is not a religion, and the focus of your program continues to be the early learning of children (as with all storytime programs); yoga and movement are simply tools that you are using to help stimulate children's early learning through physical activity and embodied play. Explaining this concept to concerned parties may help them feel more comfortable with the idea, particularly if the resistance is coming from within the library. However, in some situations it may be more appropriate to choose a name that leaves out *yoga* and instead uses words like *movement, active,* or *kinetic* to describe the program.

- *Using nontraditional channels of promotion.* Local yoga studios (especially if they are not teaching their own preschool yoga classes) may love that you are offering this kind of program and may be happy to help you spread the word to families in their network via newsletters, social media, or print flyers in their physical space. Local publications (print and online) that focus on alternative health, green living, parenting, and similar topics may also be good places to contact about listing your program or even featuring it in a story.

- *Taking your yoga storytime to outreach events.* Think about where the families you hope to attract with this program are shopping, socializing, and visiting with their children. Do these spaces host family programs or learning events? If so, these may be great places to take your yoga storytime on the road, in order to showcase what it's about for families who may not already be regular library users. Possibilities include local farm markets, health foods stores, yoga studios, and retailers who cater to children and families.

Preparing Yourself

A final component to consider as you think through the planning and implementation of your yoga storytime program is how to prepare yourself for your role as the storytime leader. Such preparation, of course, means many of the same things for a yoga storytime as it would for any storytime, such as organizing your materials, setting up the physical space, practicing new stories and songs, and so forth. However, there are a few additional ways in which you will want to prepare.

Yoga storytime is a physical program, and you will be using your body. Take the time to prepare your body for this physical activity by spending some time doing your own yoga practice or stretching routine. Though a simple warm-up song or rhyme will be enough to prepare the bodies of young children for bigger movements such as yoga poses, adult bodies tend to carry more tension and tightness than those of children and, thus, need more care when preparing for the level of physical activity that leading a yoga storytime demands. At minimum, take the time to practice in advance all the movements and yoga poses that you intend to share in your program so that you are familiar with how they feel in your body and will know how to take good care of yourself.

A yoga storytime requires you to be especially attuned to the needs of the group you are serving. No matter what has come earlier in the day, or what is waiting for you to deal with later, during the program a yoga storytime leader should be completely present. This means being welcoming and including everyone who attends, no matter what level of physical ability or yoga experience they bring with them; being observant of and responsive to the needs of the group and adjusting your plans accordingly; and being able to guide the energy of the group from the warm-up stage into the most active and energetic stage and back down into the restful and relaxed stage. To be able to do this, you may want to spend a few moments, after you've set everything up for your program and before families arrive, quietly reflecting on your intention for this program. What do you want families and children to experience or feel by participating in this program? Allow yourself to sit quietly, watching your breathing, and set this intention for yourself. A very simple and brief meditation that you may find helpful for centering yourself before leading your yoga storytime is the Three Minute Breathing Space. A guided audio recording of this meditation (and several other completely secular, beginner-level mindfulness practices) from the book *Mindfulness: An Eight-Week Plan for Finding Peace in a Frantic World* by Mark Williams and Danny Penman is available to stream for free at http://franticworld.com/free-meditations-from-mindfulness/.

Concluding Thoughts

As this chapter elucidates, planning a yoga storytime has much in common with planning any other storytime program. The focus is still on young children's early learning. Books, songs, storytelling, and digital resources are still the tools that the storytime leader uses to craft the program. The key difference is that the body is very much involved. Yoga and movement are used intentionally to stimulate young children's physical, cognitive, and social-emotional development.

As with any storytime, there will be a great variety of personal styles that influence what yoga storytime looks like in action. This chapter is not intended to corral library staff interested in offering a yoga storytime into one cookie-cutter mold of programming but, rather, to present a general framework within which individual creativity can flow freely. Your yoga storytime will be uniquely yours, and that is wonderful. Be present. Be authentic. Have fun.

Chapter Four

Basic Yoga Poses for Yoga Storytime

This chapter presents thirteen basic yoga poses and thirty-five variations, for a total of forty-eight pose descriptions that nearly anyone can share with young children in a storytime setting. The poses are presented in alphabetical order using the following format:

- Pose name
- Image
- Common English name
- Sanskrit name
- Other potential names for the pose
- Variations of the pose and potential names for the variations (when applicable)
- Movement Extension
- Early Learning Tie-In

Please know that I have taken creative liberty with the naming of the presented yoga poses, as is traditional within the field of children's yoga. Some of the names presented as options for the poses can be found in resources specific to the instruction of yoga to children; others are original. I encourage you to use your own creativity when incorporating yoga poses into your programs as well; it is fine to change the names of yoga poses to make them more accessible to children and to fit the activity you are presenting. The Sanskrit names and the common English names of the yoga poses, typically used in adult yoga classes, are presented for your reference so that you can easily find more information about the poses and how to practice them safely on your own. The Sanskrit and English names used all come from *Yoga Journal*'s "List of Yoga Poses: A–Z Asana Guide," available at www.yogajournal.com/pose-finder.

BOX 4.1

Resources for Learning More about Yoga Poses

General

Brown, Christina. *The Yoga Bible: The Definitive Guide to Yogic Postures.* London, England: Octopus Publishing Group, 2003.

Iyengar, B. K. S. *Light on Yoga.* New York: Knopf Doubleday Publishing Group, 1995.

Yoga International. "Yoga Poses," https://yogainternational.com/poses.

Yoga Journal. "List of Yoga Poses: A–Z Asana Guide," www.yogajournal.com/pose-finder.

Children

Buckley, Annie. *The Kids' Yoga Deck.* San Francisco, CA: Chronicle Books, 2003.

Cosmic Kids Yoga, "Learn All the Kids Yoga Postures," http://tinyurl.com/zvs7m89.

Flynn, Lisa. *Yoga for Children: 200+ Yoga Poses, Breathing Exercises, and Meditations for Healthier, Happier, More Resilient Children.* Avon, MA: Adams Media, 2013.

Kids Yoga Stories. "58 Fun and Easy Fun Yoga Poses for Kids," www.kidsyogastories.com/kids-yoga-poses.

Power, Teresa Anne. *The ABCs of Yoga for Kids.* Illustrated by Kathleen Rietz. Pacific Palisades, CA: Stafford House, 2009.

For editorial reasons, images are provided only for the main poses and not for the variations described (though there are some exceptions to this standard). At times, poses that are distinct from the main pose are presented as variations (such as the inclusion of Child's Pose as a variation of Seated Pose II). This has been done purposefully in order to accommodate the logistical requirements of publication. In these cases, great care has been taken to recognize that the presented variation is its own distinct pose; the English and Sanskrit names of such poses are presented to aid you in further research. See Box 4.1 for a list of recommended resources for learning more about specific yoga poses.

A Movement Extension activity accompanies each pose description. This is a simple, creative way that you, the storytime leader, can use the pose or its variations, or both, in a storytime setting to engage children in physical activity and the use of their imaginations. Similarly, an Early Learning Tie-In is provided for each pose. These activities directly engage children and caregivers in the practice of an early literacy, school readiness, or social-emotional learning skill. Suggested parent messages that communicate the intentions of these activities are also provided.

Finally, a gentle reminder that yoga is an inherently physical practice. It is important that anyone using yoga in storytimes has an honest understanding of her own physical abilities and limitations, in order to know what poses are (and are not) appropriate for her body. Though the poses presented are considered *basic,* this term is subjective; what comes easily to one person may not come easily to another. I strongly encourage anyone wanting to include yoga in storytime to attend yoga classes with a reputable Registered Yoga Teacher (RYT) in order to develop a basic understanding of the practice and how it feels in your own unique body. A great article about how to find the right yoga teacher for you is available from Yoga Alliance at www.yogaalliance.org/LearnAboutYoga/AboutYoga/Findingtherightyoga teacher. Only you can know how to best take care of your body; please do so.

BOAT

English name: Boat Pose. *Sanskrit name:* Paripurna Navasana. *Also called:* V, Cone, Canoe

To Come into Pose

Begin by sitting with your bottom on the floor, knees bent in front of you, and feet flat on the floor. Prepare to come into Boat, first by lifting one leg into the air, extending directly out from your bent knee, and then returning it to the ground. Do the same with the other leg. Hands can be on the ground next to the hips to help with balance. Next, keep the hands on the floor as you lift both feet into the air at the same time and straighten the legs (see image). A fun way to test your balance here is to lift your hands, arms extended in front of you and on either side of your legs, thumbs facing the sky and palms facing your legs. However, keep in mind that young children likely do not yet have the necessary strength in their core muscles to hold themselves here for very long, if at all. Encourage them to simply try again if they lose their balance.

Movement Extension

River Adventure. Today we're going to paddle our boats down a big river! Have everyone sit in a circle and begin by making a river shape, resting on their backs. You can play some water sounds to enhance the children's imagination of this experience. Encourage them to imagine a beautiful river as they rest. What can they see? What can they hear? After resting a bit, it's time to move. Have everyone get into their boat by coming into Boat Pose. Begin paddling down the river and call out something you can see that can be paired with a shape or a sound, such as a fish, a bird, or a tree. Here is a rhyme that you can use:

> *As my boat goes sailing by,*
> *I see a _____ with my little eye.*

Invite everyone to come out of their Boat to make that shape or sound. Then go around the circle giving each child a turn to share what she can see with her imagination and to share the shape or sound that accompanies that animal or object. You may want to have something to pass around the circle that each child can hold when it is her turn and then pass along to the next child, such as a captain's hat or a pretend oar.

Early Learning Tie-In

Boat Pose looks like the letter *V.* What other letters can you make with your body? Can you make the first letter of your name? Encourage parents to find creative ways to play with letters and their sounds in order to practice the alphabet. They can help their child write his first name and then experiment with using his body to express each letter as a physical shape.

CAT AND COW

Cat   Cow

English name: Cat Pose. *Sanskrit name:* Marjaryasana.
English name: Cow Pose *Sanskrit name:* Bitilasana
Variations: Table (can also be called Square), Table Twist, Table Balance (can also be called Lobster), Reverse Table (can also be called Spider)

These two poses are often linked, with Cow being done on the inhale and Cat on the exhale, which is why they are being described together. Feel free to use them and their variations separately.

To Come into Pose

Begin on hands and knees. To come into Cow, let the belly sink toward the ground, tilting the hips up and lifting the chin to look upward. The back now has a slight hammock shape, with the middle of the back being closer to the ground and the hips and face pointing up toward the sky (see image). To come into Cat, reverse the shape by pressing down through the hands, rounding through the upper back, and looking back between the thighs (see image). This shape resembles that of a Halloween cat.

Variations

For Table (or Square) variation: Assume the starting position for Cat and Cow, with the hands on the ground under the shoulders, the knees on the ground under the hips, and the tops of the feet on the floor with the toes pointing straight back behind you.

For Table Twist variation: From Table, keep the left hand firmly planted on the ground and sweep the right arm up to the right side. Follow the twist with your gaze. Return the right hand to the ground and repeat on the left side.

For Table Balance (or Lobster) variation: From Table, stretch one arm long in front of the body (for Lobster, it is fun to add a pinching motion with the hand here). Return the hand to the starting position and repeat on the second side.

For Reverse Table (or Spider) variation: This shape is similar to Table but with the belly facing the ceiling instead of the floor. To come into the shape, begin by sitting as though you were going to come into Boat, with hips down on the ground, knees bent in front of you, and feet flat on the floor. Place the hands on the ground under your shoulders with the fingers facing the feet. Press into the hands and the feet to lift the hips, coming into a Reverse Table. If you are using this shape as Spider, gently walk around on your "web"!

Movement Extension

Making Animal Sounds. Add a "moo" like a cow and a "meow" like a cat as you move through the Cow and Cat shapes. Try adding other animals and their sounds into this series of movements one at a time, such as Dog, Donkey (a variation of Dog), and Frog (a variation of Chair).

Early Learning Tie-In

Telling a Story with Sound. Introduce the book *Moo!* by David LaRochelle, either by showing it to the group or by playing the book trailer available at https://you tu.be/4p5889jf0t8. This title uses one single word, "Moo," to tell an entire story. Provide adults and children an opportunity to make up and tell each other their own story using just one word or sound. How else can they express what is happening when their word choices are limited? Have a selection of other wordless and nearly wordless books available for checkout, and encourage adults to use them at home. Remind adults that making up stories together and listening to children tell their own stories are great ways to help them develop early literacy skills that will aid them in their later reading comprehension.

CHAIR

English name: Fierce Pose. *Sanskrit name:* Utkatasana. *Also called:* Lightning Bolt. *Variations:* Frog, Duck

To Come into Pose
Begin in Standing Pose. Bend the knees and send the hips down behind you, as though you were sitting in an invisible chair. Sweep the arms up into the air as you hold the pose (see image).

Variations
For Frog variation: This is a form of Garland Pose, or Malasana in Sanskrit. To come into Frog from standing, take a wider stance with the legs spread a little bit wider than the hips. Bend the knees slowly, bringing the hips down toward the ground. Hands can be on the ground in front of you for balance. Make this pose more froglike by hopping in the air with a big "Ribbit!"

For Duck variation: From Frog, bring the hands up into the armpits to make wings. Flap your wings, waddle, and quack!

Movement Extension
Monkey Jumps.[1] Begin crouched down into a version of Frog with a narrow stance. Hands are on the ground near the feet. On the count of three, jump up, spreading the arms and legs wide as you are in the air and making a big monkey sound! Return to your crouched down, narrow Frog position when you land from your Monkey Jump.

Early Learning Tie-In

"Five Green and Speckled Frogs" is a traditional and well-known counting rhyme. Try sharing this rhyme while practicing a different seated pose for each verse. For example, you may want to start in Seated Pose I or II, then move with each verse into different variations of those poses, such as Staff Pose, Dragonfly Pose, and Butterfly Pose. End in Frog Pose, hopping once for each of the five little froggies that jumped into the pool.

Five Green and Speckled Frogs

Five green and speckled frogs,

Sat on a speckled log,

Eating some most delicious bugs. Yum! Yum!

One jumped into the pool,

Where it was nice and cool.

Now there are four green speckled frogs.

Continue until all the frogs have jumped into the water.

Remind adults that sharing a simple rhyme like this is a powerful way to help children build strong brains. Playing with sound and rhyme by singing helps children build important early literacy skills such as phonological awareness, and research has shown that combining such early literacy practices with movement may improve their effectiveness (see chapter 2). Counting is also an important early numeracy skill that helps children prepare for kindergarten.

DOG

English name: Downward-Facing Dog. *Sanskrit name:* Adho Mukha Svanasana. *Also called:* Zebra, Horse. Variations: Donkey, Dolphin

To Come into Pose

This is the quintessential yoga pose that many people think of when they think of yoga. The shape resembles an upside-down *V*, in which the hands and feet are on the ground, the legs and arms are long, the spine is long, and the hips are up in the air (see image). To come into the shape, begin in Table Pose, with the hands on the ground under the shoulders and the knees on the ground under the hips. Push down with your hands as you lift the hips up and back. The heels of the feet may not come all the way to the floor—this is fine! Depending on what animal name you are using, bark or neigh as you hold the pose.

Variations

For Donkey variation: From Dog Pose, lift one leg at a time up into the air.

For Dolphin variation: From Dog Pose, lower onto the forearms instead of the hands.

Movement Extension

Salute the Sun

One of the most popular series of yoga movements is the Sun Salutation, of which there are many varieties. For a gentle, child-friendly Sun Salutation, try the following movements:

Begin in Standing Pose. (1)

Breathe in and stretch the arms up overhead into Extended Mountain. (2)

Breathe out and bend at the hips to touch the toes, coming into a Forward Fold. (3)

Breathe in and step the legs back into Table Pose. (4)

Breathe out and come all the way down to the belly with your legs back behind you and your hands under your shoulders. (5)

Breathe in and lift the head and chest to come into Snake Pose. (6)

Breathe out and push back into Dog Pose. (7)

Breathe in and walk the feet forward.

Breathe out and hang down in Forward Fold. (8)

Breathe in and come back up to standing in Extended Mountain, stretching the arms overhead. (9)

Breathe out and rest your arms by your sides as you return to Standing Pose. (1)

Two songs that present fun, child-friendly versions of Sun Salutations are "Sun Dance" by Bari Koral[2] and "Dance for the Sun" from *Dance for the Sun: Yoga Songs for Kids* by Kira Willey.

Early Learning Tie-In

Talk about the word *salutation*. Ask the group to share the words and phrases they use to greet their friends, family, and neighbors, including any ways that they may know to greet people in other languages. Make a greeting game by playing music for the kids to dance to. When the music pauses, have the children pause their bodies in a way that shows they are friendly, kind, and welcoming to others. How can they express these ideas with their bodies? Then have them find someone in the group to greet by using the words and phrases you discussed. A fun book to pair with this discussion is *Say Hello!* by Rachel Isadora.

FISH

English name: Locust Pose. *Sanskrit name:* Salabhasana. *Also called:* Worm.
Variations: Shark, Whale

To Come into Pose

Begin by lying belly down with the arms along the sides of the body. At the same time, lift the legs, the chest, and the arms off the ground (see image). "Swim" like a fish by raising and lowering the arms and legs. To release the pose, let the arms, chest, head, and legs once again rest on the ground.

Variations

For Shark variation: Begin lying belly down on the ground. Clasp the hands together behind the back to make a fin and then lift the chest and legs into the air as you do in Fish.

For Whale variation (advanced): Whale is a variation of Bow Pose, or Dhanurasana in Sanskrit. To come into the pose, begin by lying belly down on the ground. Bend the knees so that the feet come up close to the hips. Clasp the ankles with the hands. Then lift the chest and legs into the air. Because this pose can be challenging for adult bodies, I recommend that storytime presenters who wish to use it have a regular yoga practice and feel comfortable coming into and out of the pose.

Movement Extension

I Swam in the Ocean and I Saw a . . . Play a game in which the children imagine they can breathe underwater. What would you see if you could swim under the ocean? Go around the group and let each child share one thing she might see while swimming under the ocean. How could the children make the shape of that object or creature with their bodies? When it's time to end the underwater adventure, swim up to the surface of the water, climb into a boat (Boat Pose), and take a rest (Rest Pose).

Early Learning Tie-In

Fishy Rhyme Time. Sit in a circle and have a soft ball that you can roll on the floor. Introduce a word, such as fish, and ask the group to think of as many words as they can that rhyme with fish. Roll the ball to someone in the circle. The person with the ball can share a rhyming word and then roll the ball to someone else. If anyone gets stuck, he can ask the group for help or pass and roll the ball to another child. When all the rhyming words have been exhausted, play the same game using another starter word that corresponds with your program theme. Remind adults that playing with sound by exploring rhyme helps prepare children to learn to read.

FORWARD FOLD

English name: Standing Forward Bend. *Sanskrit name:* Uttanasana. *Also called:* Waterfall. *Variation:* Elephant

To Come into Pose

Begin in Standing Pose with both feet flat on the floor and toes facing the same direction. Make a slight bend in the knees and fold forward, bringing the hands to the ground on either side of the feet (see image). For a little fun while you're down here, add in a tickle for the toes!

Variation

For Elephant variation: From Forward Fold, clasp the hands in front of you with the arms hanging down long in front of your body. This is your elephant trunk. Swing your trunk from side to side. For extra movement, make elephant stomps, lifting and stomping one foot at a time.

Movement Extension

Playful Elephants. Have children and caregivers sit in a big circle and sing the traditional children's song "One Elephant Went Out to Play." Have one child go into the middle of the circle, now your spider web, and make her Elephant shape. Let that child pick the next animal before returning to her place in the circle. Sing the song again, replacing elephant with the new animal. The next child can then go into the middle of the circle and make his own version of that animal shape. Shy children or children who are reluctant to participate should be welcome to bring their grown-up into the circle with them, if that makes them feel more comfortable, or to pass and simply watch.

One Elephant Went Out to Play

One elephant went out to play,
Upon a spider's web one day.
She/he had such delightful fun,
That she/he called another animal friend to come.

Continue singing, replacing *elephant* with the various animals suggested by the group until each child has had a turn.

Early Learning Tie-In

Big Animals. Elephants are big animals! As a group, brainstorm other words you can think of to describe something that is very big. Suggestions include giant, gargantuan, massive, huge, and enormous. How can the children express these ideas with their bodies? Does gargantuan look different from big? Remind parents that exposing children to lots of words helps them develop a rich vocabulary, an important skill for later learning to read. Be sure to let the adults know that sharing picture books at home with their children is a great way to encounter lots of words, including words we may not necessarily use in everyday conversation. Have some of your favorite examples of such books on display for parents and caregivers to check out and use at home.

LIZARD

English name: High Lunge. *Sanskrit name:* none. *Also called:* Newt, Chameleon, Salamander. *Variations:* Dragon (can also be called Dinosaur), Grasshopper

To Come into Pose

From Standing Pose, fold forward and place the hands on the ground. Take a big step back with one leg. Bend the front knee. The back leg is extended long, with the knee off the ground, the toes on the ground, and the heel up.

Variations

For Dragon (or Dinosaur) variation: From Lizard, lift the arms off the ground and into the air alongside the head with the palms facing each other. This pose requires a good bit of balance and may be challenging for some children (see image). See Grasshopper for a more accessible version of this pose.

For Grasshopper variation: This pose is known as Low Lunge, or Anjaneyasana in Sanskrit. From Lizard Pose, gently place the back knee to the ground. Hands can stay on the ground for balance or lift up alongside the ears for a more accessible version of Dragon Pose.

Movement Extension

Move through different variations of the poses just described as you share the following rhyme. For example, begin in Lizard on the right side. Then move to Lizard on the left side. Then move to Grasshopper on the right and left. End in Dragon on either side. Stick out your tongue to slurp up the bugs as you count down.

Lizard Play[3]

Five little bugs on the forest floor,
Along came a sticky tongue lizard . . . SLURP! Now there are four.
Four little bugs on a kapok tree,
Along came a sticky tongue lizard . . . SLURP! Now there are three.
Three little bugs without a single clue,
Along came a sticky tongue lizard . . . SLURP! Now there are two.
Two little bugs soaking up the hot sun,
Along came a sticky tongue lizard . . . SLURP! Now there is one.
One little bug knew that he was done,
Along came a sticky tongue lizard . . . SLURP! Now there are none.

Early Learning Tie-In

Talk about animal adaptations as a way to introduce science vocabulary. For example, you can talk about the ability of chameleons to change color, of newts to secrete a poison through their skin when they perceive a threat, and of salamanders to drop their tail and grow a new one. A conversation about animal adaptations is a natural opportunity to incorporate nonfiction books into your program.

REST

English name: Corpse Pose. *Sanskrit name:* Savasana. *Also called:* Line, River. *Variations:* Circle (can also be called Cocoon), Happy Baby (can also be called Pig or Bear), Bug, Belly Rest

To Come into Pose

Recline comfortably on your back, in a supine position, with your legs extended in front of you and your arms resting by your sides (see image).

Variations

For Cocoon (or Circle) variation: From Rest, bend the knees and bring them up toward the chest. Wrap your arms around your legs and bring your forehead up toward your knees, making a tight ball with the body.

For Happy Baby (also Pig or Bear) variation: This pose is known as Happy Baby, or Ananda Balasana in Sanskrit. From Rest, bend the knees and bring them into the chest. With your legs open to about hip width, raise the soles of the feet up toward the sky, making the shins perpendicular to the thighs. Reach up with your hands to grab hold of the feet and pull them down toward the body. It can feel nice for the back to rock a little from side to side.

For Bug variation: From Rest, extend the legs and the arms vertically into the air and give them all a shake!

For Belly Rest variation: Lie in a prone position, with the belly on the ground. You can bring the hands in front of the head, one on top of the other, to make a little pillow for the forehead to rest on.

Movement Extension

Wiggle and Rest. While in Rest Pose, instruct the children to wiggle various body parts one at a time and then allow them to become very still. You may choose to work from the bottom of the body to the top, wiggling and then resting the toes, the legs, the hips, and so on. This movement can be a nice way to transition the group from the activity of the storytime into a few moments of rest and stillness before they leave. Turn down the lights, play calming music, and use a gentle voice to enhance this effect. If resting on their back or belly is not comfortable, it is fine to encourage children and adults to rest in any other position that they prefer.

Early Learning Tie-In

One-on-One Reading Time. Before coming to final rest at the end of storytime, hand out some very simple books to the adults in the group and encourage them to enjoy a few minutes of individual reading time with their children. This is a great time to snuggle up, using physical closeness to communicate safety and love. Choose books that are calming and have a positive message for this experience (see chapter 3 for recommended books). Have a quiet way to signal the end of this time and make the transition to rest, such as gently ringing a bell. Remind adults that having positive experiences with books and reading helps young children develop print motivation, an early literacy skill that makes it easier for them to learn to read when they begin school.

SEATED POSE I

English name: Easy Pose. *Sanskrit name:* Sukhasana. *Also called:* Rooster, Criss-Cross, Pretzel Legs. *Variations:* Lion, Butterfly (can also be called Diamond), Clam, Turtle, Flower

To Come into Pose

Sit comfortably with legs crossed in front of you and the spine tall. Hands can rest gently on your lap or come together in front of your chest.

Variations

For Lion variation: Lion can be done from any seated position. Take a normal inhale. On the exhale, open the eyes widely, stretch out the tongue, and audibly expel the breath out like a roaring lion. The sillier you feel in this pose, the better!

For Butterfly (or Diamond) variation: Butterfly is a modified version of Bound Angle Pose, or Baddha Konasana in Sanskrit. To come into Butterfly from Seated Pose I, bring the soles of the feet together. Keep hands on your lap, or reach for feet or ankles. Gently bounce your butterfly wings up and down. To add a little more imagination, bring your hands to the sides of your forehead with soft fists and index fingers extended as antennae!

For Clam variation: From Butterfly, fold forward. Open and close like a clam by coming into and out of the fold.

For Turtle variation: From Butterfly, slip your hands under your legs, palms down, and fold forward. Feel yourself folding up like a turtle in its shell.

For Flower variation: From Butterfly, slip your hands under your legs and hold onto your ankles. Lift your legs up into the air. How long can you balance here?

Movement Extension

Butterfly Life Cycle.[4] Begin in Child's Pose, resting like an egg on a leaf. Start to wiggle and eventually move into a Caterpillar (another name for Snake Pose), stretched out belly down on the ground. Wiggle around eating leaves and other things. To make this part more interactive, invite children to call out what they are eating as caterpillars. Eventually, it's time to rest inside your Cocoon—a version of Rest Pose. See how long you can get the group to rest quietly here before bursting through the cocoon by wiggling arms and legs in the air and coming to sit in Butterfly Pose. Gently bounce your butterfly wings up and down, flying in the air, before coming to land on a flower and lifting up into Flower Pose.

Early Learning Tie-In

Shapes and Letters Guessing Game. Have the children and their adult caregivers work together in this guessing game. First, have the children come into any version of Seated Pose I that they prefer. Then have the adults sit behind their child and "draw" with their finger a shape or letter on the child's back. Can the child guess the shape or letter? After a few rounds, switch positions. Now the adult is in Seated Pose I and the child has a chance to practice "drawing" letters and shapes. Remind parents and caregivers that writing (even pretend writing!) is an important early literacy practice.

SEATED POSE II

English name: Staff Pose. *Sanskrit name:* Dandasana. *Also called:* Log. *Variations:* Dragonfly, Seated Forward Fold (can also be called Arrow), Egg (can also be called Mouse, Seed, Snail, or Oval)

To Come into Pose
Sit with your legs extended in front of you and your spine upright and tall (see image).

Variations

For Dragonfly variation: From Seated Pose II, extend the legs wide apart on the ground, making a *V* shape. Continue sitting with the spine upright.

For Seated Forward Fold (or Arrow) variation: This pose is known as Seated Forward Bend, or Paschimottanasana in Sanskrit. Begin in Seated Pose II, with the arms extended alongside the head, palms facing each other. Hinge forward from the hips, keeping the spine long, to fold forward. Arms can stay extended, rest on the legs, or reach for the toes.

For Egg (or Mouse, Seed, Snail, or Oval) variation: This pose (above) is known as Child's Pose, or Balasana in Sanskrit. To come into Egg Pose, begin by sitting with your hips on your heels; your bent knees are in front of you and your shins are beneath you. Legs can be close together or spread wide apart, depending on what feels best in the body. Fold forward, bringing your forehead to the ground. Allow the arms to rest beside the body with the hands near the feet, or extend them long in front of you, resting on the ground.

Movement Extension

Egg, Egg, Bird. This is a yoga version of "Duck, Duck, Goose." Have the children sit in a circle. Everyone begins in their Egg shape. One person walks around the circle, touching the children on the back one at a time and saying "Egg" each time, until the person says "Bird." That child then hatches from the Egg shape and chases the person, who is running around the circle to come into Egg in the now open spot. The child who was selected as bird now has a turn to play.

Early Learning Tie-In

Child's Pose (along with most seated forward folds) can be very calming. Help children experience this for themselves by practicing a few more active movements (such as Monkey Jumps or a Sun Salutation) and then practicing Child's Pose. Ask children to describe the difference in how they feel after practicing these poses. When might Child's Pose be helpful to them, outside practicing yoga? You can connect this conversation even more directly to emotions by having children and caregivers work together to brainstorm poses that they can try at home when they feel angry, sad, or hyper. Explain to adults that learning to recognize emotions, and developing tools for coping with them, helps children develop social-emotional learning skills.

SNAKE

English name: Cobra Pose. *Sanskrit name:* Bhujangasana. *Also called:* Caterpillar. *Variation:* Seal

To Come into Pose

Begin by lying belly down on the ground. Legs are straight back behind you, close together, with the fronts of all ten toes resting on the ground. Bring the hands in under the shoulders. Gently lift the chest and head off the ground, keeping the feet on the floor and the hands on the floor with the elbows bent (see image).

Variation

For Seal variation (*advanced*): From Snake Pose, press down into the hands to straighten the arms and lift the chest into a deeper backbend. Because this pose can be challenging for adult bodies, I recommend that storytime presenters who wish to use it have a regular yoga practice and feel comfortable coming into and out of the pose.

Movement Extension

"S" Is for "Snake." "Snake" starts with the letter s. Have the group help you think of other animals to accompany various letters, perhaps even matching this activity to spell out a word of the day. For example, your word of the day could be sing (also an important early literacy practice). Have the group help you think of an animal for each letter (e.g., s = snake, i = inchworm, n = newt, g = giraffe). Alternatively, you could introduce the animals and the yoga poses that accompany them and ask the group to tell you what letter the word starts with. Write the letters on a white board and say the word together. After you reveal that the word is sing, sing a song together about a snake, such as "I'm Being Swallowed by a Boa Constrictor" by Shel Silverstein. This activity can be modified to be used with any words, animals, or themes. *The ABCs of Yoga for Kids* by Teresa Anne Power is a great resource for finding child-friendly yoga poses that accompany every letter of the alphabet.

Early Learning Tie-In

The activity just described is a way to use play, one of the early literacy practices described by Every Child Ready to Read, to help children in their development of early literacy skills. Along the way, point out to parents and caregivers some of the benefits of this type of play: children are practicing letters, building vocabulary, and exploring rhyme. Remember, play is a child's work, and parents are a child's first and most important teacher!

STANDING POSE

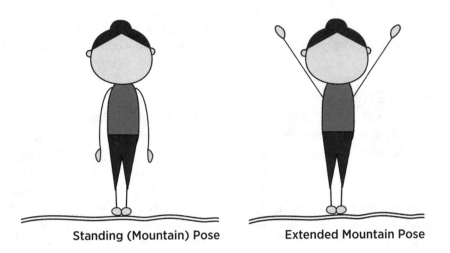

Standing (Mountain) Pose   Extended Mountain Pose

English name: Mountain Pose. *Sanskrit name:* Tadasana. *Also called:* Stick, Line. *Variations:* Extended Mountain, Giraffe, Flamingo, Crescent Moon (can also be called Rhinoceros), Star, Star Twist

To Come into Pose
Simply come to standing with the feet close together and flat on the floor with all ten toes facing forward. Arms hang gently down by your sides, and the spine is tall.

Variations
For Extended Mountain variation: From Standing Pose, lift the arms alongside the head, palms facing each other and thumbs facing behind you (see image).

For Giraffe variation: From Extended Mountain, tilt the head back and look up between the hands.

For Flamingo variation: Begin in Standing Pose with both feet flat on the floor. Bring the hands to the hips and lift one leg in front of you with the knee bent. Balance here as long as you can. Then bring the raised leg back down. Shake it out, and try again on the other side!

For Crescent Moon (or Rhinoceros) variation: This pose is known as Crescent Moon, or Chandrasana in Sanskrit. From Extended Mountain, bring the hands together above the head (this makes your horn in Rhinoceros). Keep both feet flat on the ground and bend over to one side, making a crescent moon shape. Come back to the middle and try the same shape on the other side.

For Star variation: From Standing Pose, move your feet apart to make a wider stance. Extend your arms out to the sides, directly from the shoulders. Now the head, hands, and feet make five points, like a star.

For Star Twist variation: From Star, twist and fold forward, touching one hand to the opposite foot. Come back up to center and try this twist on the other side.

Movement Extension

Happy Spines. Have caregivers help children locate their spines. Talk about the spine being an important part of the body. The bones that are here help protect the nerves and muscles that we need to run, jump, do yoga, and give hugs! To take care of the spine and keep it happy, we need to move and stretch it every day. The following movements take the spine through its full range of motion (extension, flexion, lateral bending, and twisting)—an important thing to do daily to keep the spine supple no matter your age!

Begin in Standing Pose.

Stretch up into Giraffe, looking between the hands for a gentle back bend.

Bend the knees and come into a Forward Fold.

Return to Standing Pose.

Stretch your arms over your head and come into Crescent Moon on each side.

Return to Standing Pose.

Come into Star with the arms and legs wide. Take a Star Twist on each side.

Jump the feet back together and release the arms down by your sides, ending in Standing Pose.

Early Learning Tie-In

Exploring Opposites. Use the variety of movements you can come into from Standing Pose to play with opposites. The following are some suggestions:

UP (Extended Mountain) and DOWN (Forward Fold)

WIDE (Star) and NARROW (Standing Pose)

CURVED (Crescent Moon) and STRAIGHT (Standing Pose)

LEFT (Twisted Star to the left foot) and RIGHT (Twisted Star to the right foot)

TALL (Giraffe) and SHORT (Frog)

Make this activity more interactive by inviting group participation. One child can call out a description (such as "big") and show the group her "Big Pose." Then another child can call out the opposite of that description and show the group his pose. Remind adults that talking about opposites is a great way to introduce vocabulary and help build a child's background knowledge.

TREE

English name: Tree Pose. *Sanskrit name:* Vrksasana. *Also called:* Triangle.
Variations: Extended Tree, Bending Tree, Toppling Tree (can also be called Bird)

To Come into Pose

Begin in Standing Pose with both feet flat on the floor. Keep one leg strong, with the foot flat on the floor, as you come up on the tippy toes of the other foot. Then turn that knee out to the corresponding side (i.e., if you are on the tippy toes of the left foot, now turn the left knee out to the left side). Pick up the foot and place it on the standing leg, either above or below the knee, but not on the knee (see image). Hands can be on the hips or out to the sides to help balance. This pose requires a lot of balance, which is quite tricky for children this age! Encourage them to move slowly, to stand near a wall or hold the hand of their grown-up for extra support, and to look at something on the ground in front of them that's not moving. If they wobble or fall, that's okay! Encourage them to come back and try again when they are ready and to enjoy the process rather than trying to balance perfectly. Remember to do both sides!

Variations

For Extended Tree variation: From Tree Pose, slowly lift the arms overhead.

For Bending Tree variation: From Extended Tree Pose, slowly bend from side to side. This variation can also be done with both feet on the floor.

For Toppling Tree (or Bird) variation: This pose is known as Warrior III, or Virabhadrasana III in Sanskrit. Begin in Standing Pose with both feet flat on the floor. Extend the arms up overhead, in Extended Mountain. Take a big step back with one leg, keeping the toes on the ground at first. Begin to topple over, coming into balance on the front leg, with the back leg raised behind the body and the arms extended in front of the body.

Movement Extension

Grow from a Seed to a Tree![5] Begin in Seed Pose (a variation of Seated Pose II), resting like a seed in the ground. Sprout your roots by stretching the arms forward. Sprout your stem by coming up to Seated Pose I. Grow your roots even more by stretching the legs out wide into Dragonfly (a variation of Seated Pose II). Grow even taller by bending the knees and sitting on the heels. Feel the rain nourish you as you tap on the legs, softly at first and then louder to make the sound of a rain storm. Grow even taller by sitting in a high kneeling position. Stretch the arms up overhead to make a sun shape and feel the sun helping you become stronger. Grow even taller by moving into Standing Pose. Feel the gentle breeze sway you from side to side as you come into the Bending Tree variation with both feet on the ground. Finally, come into Tree Pose, remembering to do both sides.

Early Learning Tie-In

Friendship Grove[6] After practicing Tree Pose on both sides, ask children to share what this experience was like. Was it difficult to balance on one leg? How did you feel in the pose? Turn this from an individual pose into a group pose by inviting everyone to stand close together in a circle. This time, instead of being many individual trees, you are working together to create a grove of trees. Support one another by placing arms around one another's shoulders or holding hands. Come into Tree Pose again, with everyone doing the same side at the same time. After trying both sides, talk about how this experience was different from the first. What was it like to have the support of others in the group? Did this change how you felt in the pose? What are some other situations in which having the support of others may help us feel more steady and balanced? Working together in this way can help children realize that they are not alone. When we support one another, and receive the support of others, we can feel more balanced and stable.

NOTES

1. A video demonstration of this movement is available from Cosmic Kids Yoga at https://youtu.be/oZYK40ofqK4.

2. This version of a Sun Salutation is different from the one described but still very fun to use with preschool kids. A YouTube video that shows the movements is available at https://youtu.be/g6B_OaTQm2I.

3. Rhyme found on the *Miss Hootie Hoo* blog at www.misshootiehoo.com/2011/08/storytime-theme-snakes-and-snails-and.html.

4. This activity is a modified version of the yoga sequence presented in the music video for Bari Koral's song "Butterfly," available at https://youtu.be/avHwf7yF4gg.

5. This activity is a modified version of the yoga sequence presented in the music video for Bari Koral's song "Apple Tree," available at https://youtu.be/hOOKQimko4M.

6. This activity is a modified version of the common "Forest of Trees" group yoga pose described in several sources, including in a post on the *Little Flower Yoga* blog from 2011, http://littlefloweryoga.com/blog/movement-activity-seed-to-forest-of-trees.

Chapter Five

Ready-to-Use
Yoga Storytime Plans

This chapter presents twelve yoga storytime plans. The plans are all designed to last roughly forty-five minutes as is, though they could certainly be modified to extend or shorten the time. The plans are created for a preschool-age audience, roughly three to six years old. Each plan has a title and a description that storytime presenters are welcome to use in their marketing and promotional efforts. Programs begin and end with songs and include a wide variety of books, storytelling, and songs in between. When specific yoga poses are named, the name corresponds to the name used in chapter 4 in order to make it convenient for you to locate the pose description in this book.

These programs are designed to present the storytime leader with multiple options regarding how much yoga and movement to incorporate and when. One option is simply to present the programs as described. Another is to select one or two of the movement components to use. A third option is to focus on the Featured Yoga Pose (presented in each program), perhaps incorporating the Movement Extension or Early Learning Tie-In, or both, as described in chapter 4. Rather than presenting strict mandates that must be adhered to rigidly, these program plans should be interpreted as guides for how to incorporate yoga and movement seamlessly into your storytime programs. Please make changes, move things around, and add your own ideas at will. Trust your own expertise as a storytime presenter, and allow your inner creativity to flow!

Animal Friends

Move and play with the animals!

Featured yoga pose: Elephant (a variation of Forward Fold)

Opening

Here, Here[1]
(to the tune of "Skip to My Lou")

Here, here, we're all here.
Here, here, we're all here.
Here, here, we're all here.
We're all here in storytime.

Hello, [NAME], how are you?
Hello, [NAME], how are you?
Hello, [NAME], how are you?
We're so glad to see you!

Repeat until every child has been introduced.

Movement

Walking, Walking[2]
(to the tune of "Frère Jacques")

Walking, walking. Walking, walking.
Hop, hop, hop. Hop, hop, hop.
Running, running, running. Running, running, running.
Now we stop. Now we stop.

Book
My Friends by Taro Gomi. A little girl learns from her animal friends how to move her body in various ways, such as jumping, walking, and marching.

Song
"Rockin' at the Zoo" from *Kids in the City* by Laura Doherty. Rock and move along with all the animals that are rockin' and rollin' at the zoo, including lions, monkeys, seals, penguins, and elephants.

Book
Animal Opposites: A Pop-Up Book by Petr Horáček. Try the suggested yoga poses that accompany the animals in the following chart as you explore opposites.

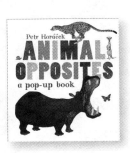

Animal	Yoga Pose
Dog	Dog Pose
Giraffe	Giraffe Pose (variation of Standing Pose)
Rabbit	Turtle Pose (variation of Seated Pose I)
Lion	Lion Pose (variation of Seated Pose I)
Pig	Happy Baby Pose (variation of Rest Pose)
Meerkat	Standing Pose
Sloth	Rest Pose
Kangaroo	Chair Pose
Hippo	Table Pose (variation of Cat and Cow Pose)
Butterfly	Butterfly Pose (variation of Seated Pose I)
Frog	Frog Pose (variation of Chair Pose)
Porcupine	Table Twist Pose (variation of Cat and Cow Pose)
Snail	Circle Pose (variation of Rest Pose)
Cheetah	Cat Pose
Mouse	Mouse Pose (variation of Seated Pose II)
Gorilla	Monkey Jumps (Movement Extension with Chair Pose)
Goose	Duck Pose (variation of Chair Pose)
Peacock	Dragonfly Pose (variation of Seated Pose II)
Ladybug	Bug Pose (variation of Rest Pose)
Elephant	Elephant Pose (variation of Forward Fold)

See the Early Learning Tie-In, "Exploring Opposites," that accompanies Standing Pose for an idea of how to use the body to further explore the concept of opposites.

Song

"Say Hi to the Animals" from *Happy Lemons by Ralph's World.* Use yoga poses and your own imagination to make shapes that go along with the animals in this song, including zebra, elephant, rhinoceros, hippopotamus, lion, and flamingo.

Book

Peace Is an Offering by **Annette LeBox.** This book introduces the idea that we live peace through our actions, in good times and in bad.

Rest

Closing

Tickle the Clouds[3]

Tickle the clouds. And tickle your toes.
Clap your hands. And tickle your nose.
Reach down low. And reach up high.
Storytime's over—wave goodbye!

~~~~~~~~~~~~~~~~~~~~~~~~~~~~~~~~~~~~~

Buggin' Out

Butterflies, bees, and other creepy-crawly critters.

Featured yoga pose: Butterfly (a variation of Seated Pose I)

OPENING

Clap as you sing, welcoming each child by name.

Let's All Clap[4]

Let's all clap 'cause [NAME] is here, [NAME] is here, [NAME] is here.
Let's all clap 'cause [NAME] is here.
[NAME] is here today!

Book

The Very Busy Spider by Eric Carle. Lots of animals try to get the spider to play, but she is too busy spinning her web to be distracted. A great story to read aloud or to share on the flannelboard.

Song

This traditional children's song will be familiar to many parents and kids. Make the movements as you sing along.

The Itsy Bitsy Spider

The itsy bitsy spider went up the water spout.
Down came the rain and washed the spider out.
Out came the sun and dried up all the rain.
And the itsy bitsy spider went up the spout again.

Sing again, this time with a great big giant spider, and try making Spider Pose (a variation of Cat and Cow Pose)!

Movement

"Bumblebee (Buzz Buzz)" from *Buzz Buzz* by Laurie Berkner. This high-energy song can be used to introduce the bug theme for the day. It provides lots of opportunities for creating your own movements, such as using egg shakers to reinforce the rhythm of the song, flying around like bees, and making "buzzing" sounds all together.

Book

Butterfly, Butterfly by Petr Horáček. Lucy looks everywhere for her butterfly friend and finds lots of bugs and other creatures along the way. The following chart shows suggested yoga poses to accompany the story.

Creature	Yoga Pose
Butterfly	Butterfly Pose (variation of Seated Pose I)
Worm	Worm Pose (another name for Fish Pose)
Spider	Spider Pose (variation of Cat and Cow Pose)
Ladybug	Bug Pose (variation of Rest Pose)
Snail	Snail Pose (variation of Seated Pose II)
Caterpillar	Caterpillar Pose (another name for Snake Pose)
Dragonfly	Dragonfly Pose (variation of Seated Pose II)

Finish the story by inviting children to lie on their backs looking up at the sky. Then come around to each child one at a time and show the butterfly surprise on the last page.

Song

"Butterfly" from *Anna and the Cupcakes* by Bari Koral
This gentle movement song introduces the life cycle of a butterfly.

Book

A Good Day by Kevin Henkes. The day seems to be going all wrong, until things suddenly turn around for the better.

Rest

Closing

This Is Big Big Big [5]

This is big big big. (Hold arms out to sides.)

This is small small small. (Cup hands together.)

This is short short short. (Hold hands with palms facing each other.)

This is tall tall tall. (Reach one hand above head.)

This is fast fast fast. (Circle fists quickly.)

This is slow slow slow. (Circle fists slowly.)

This is yes yes yes. (Nod head.)

This is no no no. (Shake head.)

Good-bye friends! It's time to go! (Wave good-bye.)

A Day at the Beach

Stories that splish, splash, and stretch!

Featured yoga pose: Whale (variation of Fish Pose)

Opening

This is a modified version of the song "Hello Everybody" from *Lullabies and Lap-Rhymes with Sally and Erika* by Sally Jaeger and Erika Webster.

Hello Everybody

Hello everybody and how are you?

How are you? How are you?

Hello everybody and how are you?

How are you today?

Hello [NAME] and how are you?

How are you? How are you?

Hello [NAME] and how are you?

How are you today?

Movement

This movement song introduces various creatures that can be found in the sea. After singing each verse, try the corresponding yoga pose.

Sharks in the Sea[6]

(to the tune of "The Wheels on the Bus")

(Stretch arms wide and clap them together to "chomp.")

The sharks in the sea go chomp, chomp, chomp.

Chomp, chomp, chomp! Chomp, chomp, chomp!

The sharks in the sea go chomp, chomp, chomp,

All day long.

Yoga pose: Shark (variation of Fish Pose)

("Pinch" fingers and thumbs together.)

The lobsters in the sea go pinch, pinch, pinch.

Pinch, pinch, pinch! Pinch, pinch, pinch!

The lobsters in the sea go pinch, pinch, pinch,
All day long.

Yoga pose: Lobster (variation of Cat and Cow Pose)

(Sit tall with legs in front of you. "Open" by lifting arms up overhead,
and "close" by folding forward over extended legs.)

The clams in the sea go open and shut.
Open and shut! Open and shut!
The clams in the sea go open and shut,
All day long.

Yoga pose: Clam (variation of Seated Pose I)

(Use your hands to pretend to "squirt" water out of a blowhole.)

The whales in the sea go squirt, squirt, squirt.
Squirt, squirt, squirt! Squirt, squirt, squirt!
The whales in the sea go squirt, squirt, squirt,
All day long.

Yoga pose: Whale (variation of Fish Pose)

Book

The Yoga Game by the Sea **by Kathy Beliveau.** This book is a yoga guessing game in which riddles are used as clues to introduce various poses. However, some of the poses introduced are a little on the advanced side (such as Rainbow, Eagle, and a different version of Fish). Think carefully about which poses to share, and skip any that you do not feel comfortable demonstrating.

Song

"I'm a Little Fish" from *In a Heartbeat* **by Laura Doherty**. Meet lots of animals that swim and play in the ocean in this movement song. Suggested movements to use along with the animals mentioned in the song are: pretending to swim (fish); Dolphin Pose, which is a variation of Dog Pose (dolphin); swaying back and forth while kneeling (seahorse); wiggling the body all around (octopus); and crawling on hands and knees (crab).

Book

Swimmy **by Leo Lionni.** Swimmy meets lots of interesting creatures as he swims through the sea. During or after reading the book, try out some yoga poses inspired by Swimmy's journey. Suggested poses are shown in the following chart.

Sea Creature	Yoga Pose
Jellyfish	Forward Fold
Lobster	Lobster Pose (variation of Cat and Cow Pose)
Strange Fish	Whale Pose (variation of Fish Pose)
Seaweed	Crescent Moon Pose (variation of Standing Pose)
Eel	Snake Pose
Sea Anemone	Tree Pose

Song

"The Goldfish" from *The Best of The Laurie Berkner Band* by **The Laurie Berkner Band.** Rest in Child's Pose when the little fish are sleeping on their rocks and then have fun acting out all the goofy movements introduced in the song.

Book

Breathe **by Scott Magoon.** A simple story to calm down and help ease the transition to rest. Take a slow, deep breath together as a group each time "Breathe" is repeated.

Rest

Closing

"Goodbye Song" from *Shining Like a Star* by **Laura Doherty.** This longer closing song is a good choice to use as you blow bubbles or hand out stickers to each child as everyone leaves the storytime area.

Down on the Farm

Moo, bark, and neigh along to farm-themed
stories and songs.

Featured yoga pose: Dog

Opening

"Hello Neighbor" from *Keep On Singing and Dancing* by Dr. Jean. This simple
movement song can be used to bring the group together at the beginning of
storytime.

Movement

This simple rhyme can be used to introduce the theme of the day, review farm
animal vocabulary, play with animal sounds, and begin to make some movement
with the body. You can use any animals you like. Suggestions that pair well with
yoga poses are duck, dog, horse, and cow. Make it more interactive by inviting the
children to suggest the animals and their movements!

Who Are the Animals That Live on the Farm?[7]

(to the tune of "Skip to My Lou")

Who are the animals that live on the farm?

Who are the animals that live on the farm?

Who are the animals that live on the farm?

And what do they say?

The duck is an animal that lives on the farm.

The duck is an animal that lives on the farm.

The duck is an animal that lives on the farm.

She says quack, quack, quack.

Book

Hurry! Hurry! by Eve Bunting. This picture-driven story introduces many
different farm animals, rushing to follow the rooster. The sparse text can be
shared as a call and response. End in Egg (a variation of Seated Pose I), waiting
to burst out of the egg like the little chick in the story exclaiming, "I'm here!"

Song

Bring new life to this traditional children's song by selecting animals that can be
turned into simple yoga poses. Suggestions are dog, horse, cow, cat, frog, and
mouse. Use a flannelboard or digital media to visually reinforce the animal vocabulary.

Old McDonald Had a Farm

Old McDonald had a farm,
E-I-E-I-O.
And on that farm he had a dog,
E-I-E-I-O.
With a bark, bark here,
And a bark, bark there.
Here a bark, there a bark,
Everywhere a bark, bark.
Old McDonald had a farm,
E-I-E-I-O.

Come into Dog Pose together as a group. Continue with other animals.

Book

Señor Pancho Had a Rancho **by René Colato Laínez.** Learn the animal sounds in English and Spanish, and try some yoga poses to go along with the animals you meet.

Song

"Back to the Farm" from T*he Apple Tree and the Honey Bee* **by Bari Koral.** Little ponies are trying to get some sleep on the farm, but the other animals keep waking them up!

Book

All in a Day **by Cynthia Rylant.** A gentle, rhyming celebration of all that can be enjoyed in a single day, one moment at a time.

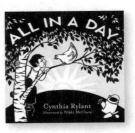

Rest

Closing

Thanks for Coming[8]
(to the tune of "My Darling Clementine")

Thanks for stretching, thanks for listening,
Thanks for coming here today!
Now that storytime is over,
Hope you have a lovely day!

Hippity Hop

Books and songs for bouncing, hopping, and jumping.

Featured yoga pose: Frog (a variation of Chair Pose)

Opening

Hands Go Up[9]
(to the tune of "Twinkle, Twinkle Little Star")

Hands go up and hands go down,
I can turn around and round.
I can jump upon two shoes.
I can listen; so can you.
I can sit, I'll show you how.
Storytime is starting now.

Movement

"Jump Up, Turn Around" from *Moving Rhymes for Modern Times* by Jim Gill.
A movement song and a game in one!

Book

Who Hops? **by Katie Davis.** Check out what animals do (and don't!) by hopping, flying, slithering, swimming, and crawling.

Song

"Clap Your Hands" from *Here Come the ABCs* by They Might Be Giants.
A great song for a movement break.

Book

Jump, Frog, Jump! **by Robert Kalan**
Add yoga poses to this classic cumulative story, and invite children to join in on the repeated "Jump, Frog! Jump!" The following chart lists suggested poses to accompany the story.

Animal or Object	Yoga Pose
Frog	Frog Pose (variation of Chair Pose)
Fish	Fish Pose
Snake	Snake Pose
Turtle	Turtle Pose (variation of Seated Pose I)
Net	Rest Pose
Basket	Egg Pose (variation of Seated Pose II)

Song

"**Five Green and Speckled Frogs**" (see the Early Learning Tie-In
for Chair Pose, page 43, for song lyrics and movement ideas)

Book

I Don't Want to Be a Frog **by Dev Petty.** A young frog learns a lesson about
being himself.

Rest

Closing

Touch Your Nose[10]

Touch your nose.
Touch your chin.
That's the way
This game begins.

Touch your eyes.
Touch your knees.
Now pretend
You're going to sneeze.

Touch your ears.
Touch your hair.
Touch your ruby lips
Right there.

Touch your elbows
Where they bend.
Jump right up and say,
"The End!"

How Do I Feel?

Using the body to explore feelings and emotions.

Featured yoga pose: Lion (a variation of Seated Pose I)

Opening
"I'm in the Mood" from *Rise and Shine* by Raffi. A fun sing-along that introduces the concept of feelings. Sing along to the recorded version or make up your own version, including actions such as reading and stretching.

Movement
"Jump, Jump" from *I'm a Rock Star* by Joanie Leeds and the Nightlights
Jump, shake, spin, and clap along to this upbeat pop tune. A great warm-up!

Book
I Am Yoga by Susan Verde. A child feels small and overwhelmed, and simple yoga poses help her find relaxation and confidence.

Song
"Silly Dance Contest" from *Jim Gill Sings the Sneezing Song and Other Contagious Tunes* by Jim Gill

Creative Movement
Feeling Faces Flannelboard. Use a flannelboard to introduce faces displaying different emotions. Have the children talk about the feelings that they are observing on each face. You may allow adults and children some one-on-one time to talk about feelings, what they feel like in their bodies, times they have felt those feelings, how they handle those feelings, and so on. You may also want to introduce some movements that we can do when we feel such feelings, as suggested in the following chart.

Feeling	Movement
Scared	Fierce Pose (another name for Chair Pose)
Happy	Spinning around, tickling toes, or any other movement that displays happiness
Sad	Giving ourselves a big hug
Mad	Lion Pose (variation of Seated Pose I)
Silly	Any silly movement that feels good

Song
"What Do I Feel" from *Breathe In: Children's Songs for Mindfulness and Awareness* by Lianne Bassin
This song is easy to move along with as it introduces children to acknowledging and processing their own emotions.

Book

The Feel Good Book **by Todd Parr.** All kinds of things feel good, like giving a hug, laughing, and sharing with others.

Rest

Closing

Bye, Good-bye[11]
(to the tune of "London Bridge")

Bye, good-bye, we'll see you soon,
See you soon, see you soon.
Bye, good-bye, we'll see you soon,
On another day.

Let's Play Yoga!

Stories and songs that introduce basic yoga poses and concepts.

Featured yoga pose: Sun Salutation (Movement Extension with Dog Pose)

Opening

Clap and Sing Hello[12]

(to the tune of "The Farmer in the Dell")

(Sing the first verse to the group as a whole.)

We clap and sing hello.
We clap and sing hello.
With our friends at storytime,
We clap and sing hello!

(Use the following verse to greet each individual child by name.)

Hello, [NAME], hello!
Hello, [NAME], hello!
We're here for yoga storytime.
Hello, [NAME], hello!

Movement

Take some time to begin by warming up your bodies with small movements, such as rotating the joints of the body (wrists, shoulders, hips, ankles, etc.) in a circle. Allow the children to suggest any further movements that might help the group warm up their bodies. Close this activity by jumping up and down as a group and shaking out the whole body.

Book

From Head to Toe **by Eric Carle.** This classic title introduces various animals accompanied by simple movements that you can act out as a group.

Song

"That's What They Do" from *Come Play Yoga!* **by Karma Kids Yoga.** This movement song also introduces various animals and their movements. All movements are explained within the song lyrics.

Book

You Are a Lion! And Other Fun Yoga Poses **by Taeeun Yoo.** This fun story is also a guessing game! Demonstrate the various movements as you read them. Can the group guess what animal each set of movements represents? Spend some time exploring each pose as it is introduced before moving on to the next.

Song

"Dance for the Sun" from *Dance for the Sun* by **Kira Willey**. This song presents a gentle, child-friendly Sun Salutation that makes a great transition for moving into the less active phase that comes toward the end of a yoga storytime. For more information about the Sun Salutation movements, see the Movement Extension activity included with Dog Pose.

Book

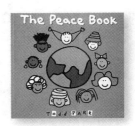

The Peace Book by **Todd Parr.** A positive book about the many ways in which we can express peace in our daily interactions with others.

Rest

Closing

Good-bye Friends

(to the tune of "Frère Jacques")

Good-bye friends. Good-bye friends.

It's time to go. It's time to go.

It always nice to see you. It's always nice to see you.

Good-bye. Good-bye.

Rhyme Time

Traditional nursery rhymes are paired
with yoga poses and movement.

Featured yoga pose: Boat

Opening

We Say Hello Like This[13]
(to the tune of "The Farmer in the Dell")

We say hello like this. (Wave.)

We say hello like this. (Wave.)

We're all here for storytime!

We say hello like this. (Wave.)

We say hello to [NAME].

We say hello to [NAME].

We're all here for storytime!

So say hello to [NAME].

Movement

"Yoga Clock (Tick Tock)" from *Come Play Yoga!* by Karma Kids Yoga.
This great warm-up song introduces various body parts. All movements are explained in the song.

Rhyme

Say this well-known nursery rhyme one time through to introduce it to the group. The second time, pair it with movement.

Hickory Dickory Dock

Hickory dickory dock. (Mouse Pose—a variation of Seated Pose II.)

The mouse ran up the clock. (Standing Pose.)

The clock struck one. (Extend one finger.)

The mouse ran down. (Forward Fold Pose.)

Hickory dickory dock. (Mouse Pose a second time.)

Rhyme

Many recorded versions of this traditional song are available. You can also pair it with a flannelboard. Suggested movement is to add Monkey Jumps (Movement Extension explained along with Chair Pose) as you count the monkeys together before each verse.

Five Little Monkeys

Five little monkeys swinging in the tree,
Teasing Mr. Crocodile, "You can't catch me!"
Along came the crocodile quiet as can be
And SNAPPED that monkey right out of the tree!

(Continue with the remaining numbers.)

Book

Row, Row, Row Your Boat **by Jane Cabrera.** Make the various animal noises together as you sail down the river in your boat. Try adding the yoga poses that match the various animals if you like.

Song

Come into Boat Pose and row from side to side as you sing this traditional song. For an added challenge, try singing as a round while you hold the pose!

Row, Row, Row Your Boat

Row, row, row your boat,
Gently down the stream.
Merrily, merrily, merrily, merrily,
Life is but a dream.

Song

Sing this song twice. The first time, make the traditional hand movements to accompany the song. The second time, come into Star Pose (variation of Standing Pose). Open and close your hands to make the "twinkle" of the star as you sing.

Twinkle, Twinkle Little Star

Twinkle, twinkle little star, how I wonder what you are.
Up above the world so high, like a diamond in the sky.
Twinkle, twinkle little star, how I wonder what you are.

Book

Nighty-Night, Cooper **by Laura Numeroff.** A mama kangaroo makes up lullabies from the tunes of familiar nursery rhymes to lull her son to sleep.

Rest

Closing

"Goodbye Children" from *Tickles and Tunes* by Kathy Reid-Naiman

Shapes Everywhere

Stories, songs, and yoga poses that introduce basic shapes.

Featured yoga pose: Crescent Moon (a variation of Standing Pose)

Opening

This great opening rhyme individually welcomes each child to storytime.

Hello! How Are You?[14]

Hello [NAME]!

How are you?

Stand up tall, we'll clap for you!

Movement

This simple rhyme incorporates gentle stretches and prepares the body for movement.

We Stretch Up High Like This
(to the tune of "The Farmer in the Dell")

We stretch up high like this.

We stretch up high like this.

We stretch up high and touch the sky.

We stretch up high like this.

Continue with the following verses and movements:

We hang down low and tickle our toes . . .

Bend side to side to move and glide . . .

We twist and turn, we listen and learn . . .

Book

Shape Shift **by Joyce Hesselberth.** A fun book that uses the imagination to play with shapes, including some less common shapes such as trapezoid and semicircle. Invite the children to draw the shapes in the air with their hands and then act out the characters created with the shapes. Suggested yoga poses to include are shown in the following chart.

Object	Yoga Pose
Ballerina	Triangle Pose (another name for Tree Pose)
Elephant	Elephant Pose (variation of Forward Fold)
Bull	Cow Pose
Fish	Fish Pose
Lady	Standing Pose
Car	Table Pose (variation of Cat and Cow Pose)
Clown	Bug Pose (variation of Rest Pose)

Note: It may be tempting to try Headstand to accompany the clown at the end of the book; please don't. Headstand is an advanced pose and is not appropriate for a library or preschool storytime setting.

Song

"The Shape Shake" from *Move It!* **by CJ.** A song and a game in one! Kids practice drawing lots of different shapes in the air to the rhythm of the song.

Movement

Use a flannelboard to introduce and name different shapes. Talk about the various shapes and then see if you can make them with your bodies. Depending on the size of your group, you could let the children add the shapes to the flannelboard one at a time. If you'd like to add a song to the movement, a good choice is "A Circle Is a Shape," sung to the tune of "The Wheels on the Bus."[15]

Movement

Play the "Shapes and Letters Guessing Game" that is described as the Early Learning Tie-In along with Seated Pose I (page 52)

Book

Whoever You Are by Mem Fox. A reminder that though we may be different, we all laugh, cry, and love the same.

Rest

Closing

The More We Get Together

The more we get together, together, together,

The more we get together,

The happier we will be.

For your friends are my friends,

And my friends are your friends.

The more we get together,

The happier we will be.

Spring Has Sprung

Welcome the arrival of spring through stories, songs, and stretches.

Featured yoga pose: Flower (a variation of Seated Pose I)

Opening

Welcome, Everyone [16]

(to the tune of "Twinkle, Twinkle Little Star")

Welcome, welcome everyone.
Now that you're here, we'll have some fun.
First we'll clap our hands just so.
Then we'll bend and touch our toe.
Welcome, welcome everyone.
Now that you're here, we'll have some fun.

Movement

This well-known children's classic helps warm up the body. Try singing it several times, mixing it up by going fast and slow.

Head, Shoulders, Knees, and Toes

Head, shoulders, knees, and toes,
Knees and toes.
Head, shoulders, knees, and toes,
Knees and toes.
Eyes, and ears, and mouth, and nose.
Head, shoulders, knees, and toes,
Knees and toes.

Book

Over in the Meadow **by Jane Cabrera.** A counting rhyme picture book that introduces lots of animals. Try making the animals' movements with your body. Add accompanying yoga poses if you wish.

Movement

Blooming Flower. Use your body to tell a story of a blooming flower. First, dig the soil (come into Chair Pose and pretend to dig). Then plant your seeds (Seed Pose—a variation of Seated Pose II). Then wait for the rain (sit on heels and tap legs to make a rain sound) and the sun (stretch arms up overhead in a circle). Start to sprout (rise up to higher kneeling position). Grow your roots (Dragonfly Pose—a variation of Seated Pose II). Finally, your flower is ready to bloom (Flower Pose—a variation of Seated Pose I)!

Book

Rachel's Day in the Garden by Giselle Shardlow. Yoga poses are incorporated into the illustrations and text of this story.

Song

"Sun Dance (Salutation)" from *Musical Yoga Adventures* by Linda Lara. An upbeat and slow Sun Salutation song.

Book

I Know the River Loves Me / Yo sé que el río me ama by Maya Christian Gonzalez. A young girl cares for the river and receives its love as the seasons change.

Rest

Closing

We Had a Good Day![17]

(to the tune of "La Cucaracha")

We had a good day! We had a great day!
So pat yourself on the back!
We had a good day! We had a great day!
So pat yourself on the back!

We stretched a lot today! We moved in many ways!
So give yourself a great big hug!
We stretched a lot today! We moved in many ways!
So give yourself a great big hug!

It's time to say so long, and end with a song!
Say good-bye to all your friends!
It's time to say so long, and end with a song!
Say good-bye to all your friends!

Strong and Mighty Trees

Exploring balance and learning about the life cycle of trees.

Featured yoga pose: Tree

Opening

We're Here for Stories and Yoga!

(to the tune of "Let's All Go to the Lobby")

(Go around the circle asking each child to say his or her name
and singing this song until all children have been welcomed.)

[NAME] is here for stories and yoga,

[NAME] is here for stories and yoga,

[NAME] is here for stories and yoga,

Who else is here today?

(When singing for the final child, close with this verse.)

[NAME] is here for stories and yoga,

[NAME] is here for stories and yoga,

[NAME] is here for stories and yoga,

Let's all have fun today!

Movement

Sing the following song, beginning in any seated position.

I'm a Tree, I Have Four Needs[18]

(to the tune of "Skip to My Lou")

I'm a tree, I have four needs.

I'm a tree, I have four needs.

I'm a tree, I have four needs.

Do you know what they are?

(Extend arms overhead, making a circle for the sun.)

I need lots and lots of sun,

I need lots and lots of sun,

I need lots and lots of sun,

To grow big and strong.

(Continue with the following verses and accompanying movements.)

I need water now and then . . .

(Take arms up overhead and bring them down in front of the body
while wiggling the fingers to make rain.)

I need air just like you . . .

(Bend from side to side to make wind.)

I need soil for my roots . . .

(Stretch the legs wide like roots and tap the ground between and around them.)

Story

Ten Red Apples **by Pat Hutchins.** This story can be shared in many different
ways. The most obvious is to read the book and either act out the animal movements or make the animal sounds that accompany the characters in the book.
This story also works very well on the flannelboard, and patterns can easily be
found online. I suggest using the flannelboard and cutting the story down from
ten apples to five, making the following animal poses and sounds:

Cow Pose

Duck Pose (variation of Chair Pose)

Horse Pose (another name for Dog Pose)

Pig Pose (variation of Rest Pose)

Rooster Pose (another name for Seated Pose I)

Tree Pose

Movement

Before sharing this rhyme, introduce the various poses that go with it:

Bird Pose (variation of Tree Pose)

Bee Sound (Make a "buzz" sound as you breathe out through the mouth.)

Snake Pose

Monkey Jumps (Movement Extension included with Chair Pose)

Tree Pose

Repeat the rhyme twice in order to do the asymmetrical poses (Bird and Tree) on
each side.

A Tree Is a Home[19]

A tree may be a home for bird.

A tree may be a home for bee.

A tree may be a home for snake.

A tree may be a home for monkey.

Hmmm. Would a tree would be a good home for me?

Book

Call Me Tree / Llámeme árbol by **Maya Christina Gonzalez.** This bilingual and gender-neutral book presents a child growing from seed to tree, connecting to a forest of trees made up of diverse children. The expressive images and sparse text allow plenty of opportunities for incorporating creative movements as you read each page aloud.

Song

"Apple Tree" from *The Apple Tree and the Honey Bee* by **Bari Koral Family Rock Band.** In this sweet song, a little seed waits for just enough rain and sun to come down so it can grow into an apple tree.

Book

I Love Our Earth by **Bill Martin Jr.** This book uses real photographs of people and landscapes from around the world to celebrate the beauty of the earth and its various seasons.

Rest

Closing

Have children sit in a circle and shake the hand of their neighbor one by one until the handshake goes around the entire circle as you sing this good-bye song.

Now It's Time to Say Good-bye

(to the tune of "Here We Go 'Round the Mulberry Bush")

Now it's time to say good-bye,

Say good-bye, say good-bye.

Now it's time to say good-bye,

We're done with storytime.

(At the end, shout together:)

See you next time!

Yoguitos

Bilingual yoga storytime fun.

Featured yoga pose: La oruga / Caterpillar (another name for Snake Pose)

Opening   **We're Here for Stories and Yoga / Cuentos, canciones y yoga**

(to the tune of "Let's All Go to the Lobby")

We're here for stories and yoga.

We're here for stories and yoga.

We're here for stories and yoga.

Let's have fun today!

Cuentos, canciones y yoga.

Cuentos, canciones y yoga.

Cuentos, canciones y yoga.

¡Vamos a divertirnos hoy!

Movement

La cicla de vida de una mariposa / Butterfly Life Cycle. This activity explores the life cycle of a butterfly. Add a visual element by using the flannelboard or images from a nonfiction book. The following chart shows key movements.

English Word	Spanish Word	Yoga Pose
Egg	el huevo	Egg Pose (variation of Seated Pose II)
Caterpillar	la oruga	Caterpillar Pose (another name for Snake Pose)
Cocoon	el capullo	Circle Pose (variation of Rest Pose)
Butterfly	la mariposa	Butterfly Pose (variation of Seated Pose I)

Book

Mariposa, mariposa by **Petr Horáček.** Spanish translation of the *Butterfly, Butterfly* book described in the "Buggin' Out" program plan.

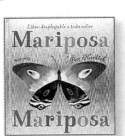

Song

"Muévete" from *From Here to There* by **Nathalia.** Clap, spin, and jump along with this upbeat bilingual tune!

Book

Moví la mano / I Moved My Hand by **Jorge Luján.** This beautiful bilingual poem celebrates the imagination and provides many opportunities for creative

movement. The following chart shows some suggested yoga poses to accompany the text.

English Word	Spanish Word	Yoga Pose
Lake	el lago	Rest Pose
Fish	el pez	Fish Pose
Moon	la luna	Crescent Moon Pose (variation of Standing Pose)
Sky	el cielo	Extended Mountain Pose (variation of Standing Pose)

Song

"**Follow the Leader / Sigue al líder**" from *Bilingual Preschool: English–Spanish* by **Sara Jordan Publishing**. Gallop like a horse, waddle like a duck, hop like a frog, and fly like a bird! ¡Galopa como un caballo, camina como un pato, brinca como una rana, y vuela como un pájaro! Act out the motions as you listen to the song and then try the corresponding yoga poses shown in the following chart.

English Word	Spanish Word	Yoga Pose
Horse	el caballo	Horse Pose (another name for Dog Pose)
Duck	el pato	Duck Pose (variation of Chair Pose)
Frog	la rana	Frog Pose (variation of Chair Pose)
Bird	el pájaro	Bird Pose (variation of Tree Pose)

Book

Gracias / Thanks by **Pat Mora**. A child contemplates many simple reasons for feeling gratitude.

Rest

Closing

**It's Time to Say Good-bye to All Our Friends /
Es tiempo a decir adiós** [20]

(to the tune of "She'll Be Coming 'Round the Mountain")

It's time to say good-bye to all our friends.
It's time to say good-bye to all our friends.
It's time to say good-bye, it's time to say good-bye,
It's time to say good-bye to all our friends.

Es tiempo a decir adiós a los amigos.
Es tiempo a decir adiós a los amigos.
Es tiempo a decir adiós, es tiempo a decir adiós,
Es tiempo a decir adiós a los amigos.

NOTES

1. Katie Salo, "Opening/Closing Songs," *Storytime Katie* (blog), https://storytimekatie.com/songs-rhymes/openingclosing-songs/.

2. National Institute of Environmental Health Services, "The Walking Song," http://kids.niehs.nih.gov/games/songs/childrens/walking-song/index.htm.

3. Verona Public Library, "Opening and Closing Songs," *Verona Storytime* (blog), http://veronastorytime.com/opening-and-closing-songs/.

4. "Let's All Clap: Storytime Welcome Song," *Jbrary*, https://youtu.be/_MDSPTqfR40.

5. Melissa Depper, "Weekly Storytime Songs," *Mel's Desk* (blog), http://melissa.depperfamily.net/blog/?page_id=378.

6. Katie Scherrer, "Bilingual Storytime Flannel Friday—Los tiburones en la mar," *¡Es divertido hablar dos idiomas!* (blog), http://bilingualchildrensprogramming.blogspot.com/2012/05/bilingual-storytime-flannel-friday-los.html.

7. "Music and Songs: Animals: Farm," *Preschool Education,* accessed August 31, 2016, www.preschooleducation.com/sfarm.shtml.

8. "Hello/Goodbye Songs," *Literary Hoots* (blog), www.literaryhoots.com/p/hello goodbye-songs.html.

9. Ibid.

10. "Closing Songs," *Miss Meg's Storytime* (blog), http://missmegsstorytime.com/storytime/closing-songs/.

11. King County Library System, "Bye Goodbye," *Tell Me a Story* (wiki), http://tmas.kcls.org/bye-goodbye/. Includes lyrics and a video demonstration.

12. Katie Salo, "Opening/Closing Songs," *Storytime Katie* (blog), https://storytimekatie.com/songs-rhymes/openingclosing-songs/.

13. Verona Public Library, "Opening and Closing Songs," *Verona Storytime* (blog), http://veronastorytime.com/opening-and-closing-songs/.

14. King County Library System, "Hello, (name)! How Are You?," *Tell Me a Story* (wiki), accessed August 31, 2016, http://kcls.org/content/hello-name-how-are-you/.

15. "A Circle Is a Shape: Storytime Song," *Jbrary*, https://youtu.be/cHUg4QuTmyc.

16. Virginia Tebo, "Storytime Openings and Closings," *Public Library Program Ideas* (wiki), http://ysostorytime.pbworks.com/w/page/6334313/Storytime%20 0penings%20and%20Closings.

17. Anne McKernan, "Opening and Closing Songs for Story Time!," *Library Adventure* (blog), www.libraryadventure.com/opening-closing-songs-for-story-time/.

18. Katie Salo, "Trees!," *Storytime Katie* (blog), https://storytimekatie.com/2013/09/02/trees/.

19. Ibid.

20. Jamie Campbell Naidoo and Katie Scherrer, *Once Upon a Cuento: Bilingual Storytimes in English and Spanish* (Chicago, IL: American Library Association, 2016), 78.

Chapter Six

Recommended Resources for Yoga Storytime Programing

This chapter provides lists of recommended print and digital materials for children's librarians and others interested in developing yoga storytime programs. A bibliography is included of all materials used in the sample yoga storytime plans. Additional recommended picture books for yoga storytime are also listed.

Professional Resources

Bersma, Danielle, and Marjoke Visscher. *Yoga Games for Children: Fun and Fitness with Postures, Movements and Breath*. Illustrated by Alex Kooistra. Alameda, CA: Hunter House, 2003.

Buckley, Annie. *The Kids' Yoga Deck*. San Francisco, CA: Chronicle Books, 2003.

Campana, Kathleen, J. Elizabeth Mills, and Saroj Nadkarni Ghoting. *Supercharged Storytimes: An Early Literacy Planning and Assessment Guide*. Chicago, IL: American Library Association, 2016.

Connell, Gill, and Cheryl McCarthy. *A Moving Child Is a Learning Child: How the Body Teaches the Brain to Think*. Minneapolis, MN: Free Spirit Publishing, 2014.

Dietzel-Glair, Julie. *Books in Motion: Connecting Preschoolers with Books through Art, Games, Movement, Music, Playacting, and Props*. Chicago, IL: American Library Association, 2013.

Flynn, Lisa. *Yoga for Children: 200+ Yoga Poses, Breathing Exercises, and Meditations for Healthier, Happier, More Resilient Children*. Avon, MA: Adams Media, 2013.

Garabedian, Helen. *Itsy Bitsy Yoga for Toddlers and Preschoolers: 8-Minute Routines to Help Your Child Grow Smarter, Be Happier, and Behave Better.* Cambridge, MA: Da Capo Press, 2008.

Ghoting, Saroj Nadkarni and Kathi Fling Klatt. *STEP into Storytime: Using StoryTime Effective Practice to Strengthen the Development of Newborns to Five-Year-Olds.* Chicago, IL: American Library Association, 2014.

Guber, Tara, and Leah Kalish. *Yoga Pretzels: 50 Fun Yoga Activities for Kids and Grownups.* Cambridge, MA: Barefoot Books, 2005.

Harper, Jennifer Cohen. *Little Flower Yoga for Kids: A Yoga and Mindfulness Program to Help Your Child Improve Attention and Emotional Balance.* Oakland, CA: New Harbinger Publications, 2013.

Namaste Kid, LLC. *Once Upon a Mat: 9 Easy-to-Learn Yoga Adventures.* DVD. 2012.

Power, Teresa Anne. *The ABCs of Yoga for Kids.* Illustrated by Kathleen Rietz. Pacific Palisades, CA: Stafford House, 2009.

Schiller, Pam. *Start Smart: Building Brain Power in the Early Years.* Lewisville, NC: Gryphon House, 2012.

Snel, Eline. *Sitting Still Like a Frog: Mindfulness Exercises for Kids (and Their Parents).* Boston, MA: Shambhala Publications, 2013.

Solis, Sydney. *Storytime Yoga: Teaching Yoga to Children through Story.* Photographs by Michele Trapani. Boulder, CO: The Mythic Yoga Studio, 2006.

Wenig, Marsha. *YogaKids: Educating the Whole Child through Yoga.* Photographs by Susan Andrews. New York: Stewart, Tabori and Chang, 2003.

Online Resources

COSMIC KIDS YOGA

www.cosmickids.com

The companion website for a popular YouTube program hosted by an English children's yoga teacher named Jamie.

EVERY CHILD READY TO READ

www.everychildreadytoread.org

A parent education initiative designed to help librarians and others teach parents about early literacy. This initiative is widely implemented in public libraries across the United States. It was first developed by the Public Library Association (PLA) and the Association for Library Service to Children (ALSC) in 2004.

KIDS YOGA STORIES

www.kidsyogastories.com

An extensive resource of ideas for sharing yoga with children founded by the author of the Kids Yoga Stories series, Giselle Shardlow.

YOGA ALLIANCE
www.yogaalliance.org
The largest nonprofit, professional organization representing the yoga community. Offers standards and certifications for yoga teachers and schools.

YOGA INTERNATIONAL
https://yogainternational.com
An organization that provides extensive education about yoga practice and teaching.

YOGA JOURNAL
www.yogajournal.com
An international organization dedicated to promoting yoga and the yoga lifestyle, best known for its magazine by the same name.

YOGIBRARIAN BLOG
https://yogibrarian.wordpress.com
Children's librarian and yoga teacher Andrea Cleland shares many storytime ideas, including program plans from her yoga storytimes.

Materials Used in Sample Storytimes

All the CDs and books used in the sample yoga storytime plans in chapter 5 are listed in this section. Also listed are recommended picture books for yoga storytime that are not included in the program plans.

MUSIC CDS
Bari Koral Family Rock Band. *Anna and the Cupcakes.* Loopytunes, 2012, compact disc.
———. *The Apple Tree and the Honey Bee.* Bari Koral, 2014, compact disc.
Bassin, Lianne. *Breathe In: Children's Songs for Mindfulness and Awareness.* Lianne Bassin, 2015, digital music.
Berkner, Laurie. *Buzz Buzz.* Razor and Tie, 2004, compact disc.
———. *The Best of the Laurie Berkner Band.* Razor and Tie, 2010, compact disc.
CJ. *Move It!* CD Baby, 2016, compact disc.
Doherty, Laura. *Kids in the City.* CD Baby, 2009, compact disc.
———. *Shining Like a Star.* CD Baby, 2011, compact disc.
———. *In a Heartbeat.* CD Baby, 2014, compact disc.
Feldman, Dr. Jean. *Keep On Singing and Dancing.* Music Design, 2007, compact disc.
Gill, Jim. *Moving Rhymes for Modern Times.* Jim Gill Music, 2006, compact disc.
———. *Jim Gill Sings the Sneezing Song and Other Contagious Tunes—20th Anniversary Edition.* Jim Gill Music, 2013, compact disc.

Jaeger, Sally, and Erika Webster. *Lullabies and LapRhymes with Sally and Erika.* CD Baby, 2007, compact disc.

Joanie Leeds and the Nightlights. *I'm a Rock Star.* Limbostar, 2010, compact disc.

Karma Kids Yoga. *Come Play Yoga!* CD Baby, 2008, compact disc.

Lara, Linda. *Musical Yoga Adventures.* Discmaker, 2007, compact disc.

Nathalia. *From Here to There.* CD Baby, 2012, compact disc.

Raffi. *Rise and Shine.* Rounder, 1998, compact disc.

Ralph's World. *Happy Lemons.* Minty Fresh, 2002, compact disc.

Reid-Naiman, Kathy. *Tickles and Tunes.* CD Baby, 2007, compact disc.

Sara Jordan Publishing. *Bilingual Preschool: Songs That Teach English–Spanish.* CD Baby, 2016, compact disc.

They Might Be Giants. *Here Come the ABCs.* Disney Sound, 2005, compact disc.

Willey, Kira. *Dance for the Sun: Yoga Songs for Kids.* Fireflies Records, 2006, compact disc.

PICTURE BOOKS

Beliveau, Kathy. *The Yoga Game by the Sea.* Illustrated by Denise Holmes. Vancouver, BC, Canada: Simply Read Books, 2015.

Bunting, Eve. *Hurry! Hurry!* Illustrated by Jeff Mack. Boston, MA: Houghton Mifflin Harcourt, 2007.

Cabrera, Jane. *Over in the Meadow.* New York: Holiday House, 2000.

———. *Row, Row, Row Your Boat.* New York: Holiday House, 2014.

Carle, Eric. *The Very Busy Spider.* New York: Penguin Young Readers Group, 1985.

———. *From Head to Toe.* New York: HarperCollins, 1997.

Davis, Katie. *Who Hops?* Boston, MA: Houghton Mifflin Harcourt, 2001.

Fox, Mem. *Whoever You Are.* Illustrated by Leslie Staub. Boston, MA: Houghton Mifflin Harcourt, 1997.

Gomi, Taro. *My Friends.* San Francisco, CA: Chronicle Books, 1995.

Gonzalez, Maya Christina. *Call Me Tree / Llámame árbol.* New York: Lee and Low, 2014.

———. *I Know the River Loves Me / Yo sé que el río me ama.* San Francisco, CA: Children's Book Press, 2009.

Henkes, Kevin. *A Good Day.* New York: HarperCollins, 2007.

Hesselberth, Joyce. *Shape Shift.* New York: Henry Holt, 2016.

Horáček, Petr. *Butterfly, Butterfly: A Book of Colors.* Somerville, MA: Candlewick Press, 2007.

———. *Mariposa, mariposa.* Madrid, Spain: S.A. Kokinos, 2007.

Hutchins, Pat. *Ten Red Apples.* New York: HarperCollins, 2000.

Kalan, Robert. *Jump, Frog, Jump!* Illustrated by Byron Barton. New York: HarperCollins, 1995.

Laínez, René Colato. *Señor Pancho Had a Rancho.* Illustrated by Ellwood Smith. New York: Holiday House, 2013.

LeBox, Annette. *Peace Is an Offering*. Illustrated by Stephanie Graegin. New York: Penguin Young Readers Group, 2015.

Lionni, Leo. *Swimmy*. New York: Random House Children's Books, 1963.

Luján, Jorge. *Moví la mano / I Moved My Hand*. Illustrated by Mandana Sadat. Translated by Elisa Amado. Toronto, ON, Canada: Groundwood Books, 2014.

Magoon, Scott. *Breathe*. New York: Simon and Schuster/Paula Wiseman Books, 2014.

Martin, Bill, Jr., and Michael Sampson. *I Love Our Earth*. Photographs by Dan Lipow. Watertown, MA: Charlesbridge Publishing, 2009.

Mora, Pat. *Gracias / Thanks*. Illustrated by John Parra. New York: Lee and Low, 2005.

Numeroff, Laura. *Nighty-Night, Cooper*. Illustrated by Lynn Munsinger. Boston, MA: Houghton Mifflin Harcourt, 2013.

Parr, Todd. *The Peace Book*. New York: Little, Brown Books for Young Readers, 2004.

———. *The Feel Good Book*. New York: Little, Brown, 2009.

Petty, Dev. *I Don't Want to Be a Frog*. Illustrated by Mike Boldt. New York: Random House Children's Books, 2015.

Rylant, Cynthia. *All in a Day*. Illustrated by Nikki McClure. New York: Abrams, 2009.

Shardlow, Giselle. *Rachel's Day in the Garden: A Kids Yoga Spring Colors Book*. Illustrated by Hazel Quintanilla. North Charleston, SC: CreateSpace Independent Publishing Platform, 2014.

Verde, Susan. *I Am Yoga*. Illustrated by Peter H. Reynolds. New York: Abrams Books for Young Readers, 2015.

Yoo, Taeeun. *You Are a Lion! And Other Fun Yoga Poses*. New York: Penguin Young Readers Group, 2012.

SUPPLEMENTAL PICTURE BOOKS

Arena, Jen. *Marta! Big and Small*. Illustrated by Angela Dominguez. New York: Roaring Brook Press, 2016.

Balouch, Kristen. *The Little Little Girl with the Big Big Voice*. New York: Little Simon, 2011.

Baptise, Baron. *My Daddy Is a Pretzel: Yoga for Parents and Kids*. Illustrated by Sophie Fatus. Cambridge, MA: Barefoot Books, 2004.

Beliveau, Kathy. *The Yoga Game*. Illustrated by Farida Zaman. Vancouver, BC, Canada: Simply Read Books, 2012.

Costello, David Hyde. *I Can Help*. New York: Farrar, Straus and Giroux, 2010.

Cotton, Katie. *Counting Lions: Portraits from the Wild*. Illustrated by Stephen Walton. Somerville, MA: Candlewick Press, 2015.

Cousins, Lucy. *Hooray for Fish!* Somerville, MA: Candlewick Press, 2005.

Craig, Lindsay. *Dancing Feet!* Illustrated by Marc Brown. New York: Random House Children's Books, 2010.

Cronin, Doreen. *Stretch*. Illustrated by Scott Menchin. New York: Simon and Schuster Children's Publishing, 2009.

Dahl, Michael. *Little Monkey Calms Down.* Illustrated by Oriol Vidal. North Mankato, MN: Picture Window Books, 2014.

Falwell, Cathryn. *Scoot!* New York: HarperCollins, 2008.

Fischer, Scott M. *Jump!* New York: Simon and Schuster Books for Young Readers, 2010.

Halperin, Wendy Anderson. *Peace.* New York: Simon and Schuster Children's Publishing, 2013.

Henkes, Kevin. *Little White Rabbit.* New York: HarperCollins, 2011.

———. *Waiting.* New York: HarperCollins, 2015.

Isadora, Rachel. *Say Hello!* New York: Penguin Young Readers Group, 2010.

Katz, Karen. *The Colors of Us.* New York: Henry Holt, 1999.

———. *Can You Say Peace?* New York: Henry Holt, 2006.

Krishmaswami, Uma. *The Happiest Tree: A Yoga Story.* Illustrated by Ruth Jeyaveeran. New York: Lee and Low, 2002.

Krosoczka, Jarrett J. *It's Tough to Lose Your Balloon.* New York: Random House Children's Books, 2015.

LaRochelle, David. *Moo!* Illustrated by Mike Wohnoutka. New York: Bloomsbury USA, 2013.

Liu, Sylvia. *A Morning with Grandpa.* Illustrated by Christina Forshay. New York: Lee and Low, 2016.

Norman, Kim. *Still a Gorilla!* Illustrated by Chad Geran. New York: Scholastic, 2016.

Page, Robin. *Move!* Illustrated by Steve Jenkins. Boston, MA: Houghton Mifflin Harcourt, 2006.

Pajalunga, Lorena V. *Yoga for Kids: Simple Animal Poses for Any Age.* Illustrated by Anna Forlati. Park Ridge, IL: Albert Whitman, 2015.

Radunsky, Vladimir. *What Does Peace Feel Like?* New York: Simon and Schuster Children's Publishing, 2004.

Rosenthal, Amy Krouse. *I Wish You More.* Illustrated by Tom Lichtenheld. San Francisco, CA: Chronicle Books, 2015.

Stein, David Ezra. *Pouch!* New York: Penguin Young Readers Group, 2009.

Thompson, Lauren. *Hop, Hop, Jump!* Illustrated by Jarrett J. Krosoczka. New York: Margaret K. McElderry Books, 2012.

Urban, Linda. *Mouse Was Mad.* Illustrated by Henry Cole. New York: Houghton Mifflin Harcourt, 2009.

Van Hout, Mies. *Playground.* New York: Lemniscaat USA, 2016.

Walsh, Ellen Stoll. *Balancing Act.* New York: Beach Lane Books, 2010.

Whitford, Rebecca. *Little Yoga: A Toddler's First Book of Yoga.* Illustrated by Martina Selway. New York: Henry Holt, 2005.

Williams, Sam. *That's Love.* Illustrated by Mique Moriuchi. New York: Holiday House, 2006.

Williams, Sue. *I Went Walking.* Illustrated by Julie Vivas. St. Louis, MO: Turtleback Books, 1992.

Wong, Janet S. Twist: *Yoga Poems.* Illustrated by Julie Paschkis. New York: Margaret K. McElderry Books, 2007.

Index

Titles of books and CDs are shown in italic.

Titles of songs and rhymes are shown in quotes.